Family Walks in Hampshire
in and around the
Meon Valley

Louis Murray

Published by Sigma Leisure – an imprint of Sigma Press, Stobart House, Pontyclerc, Penybanc Road, Ammanford, Carmarthenshire SA18 3HP.

British Library Cataloguing in Publication Data
A CIP record for this book is available from the British Library.

ISBN: 978-1-85058-930-3

Typesetting and Design by: Sigma Press, Ammanford, Carmarthenshire

Cover photograph: Louis Murray

Photographs: © Louis Murray

Maps: © Rebecca Terry

Printed by: TJ International Ltd, Padstow, Cornwall

Disclaimer: the information in this book is given in good faith and is believed to be correct at the time of publication. No responsibility is accepted by either the author or publisher for errors or omissions, or for any loss or injury howsoever caused. Only you can judge your own fitness, competence and experience. Do not rely solely on sketch maps for navigation: we strongly recommend the use of appropriate Ordnance Survey (or equivalent) maps.

Contents

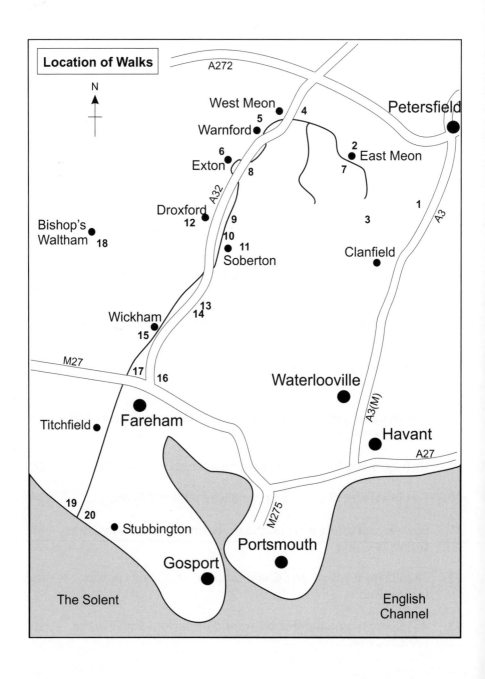

Acknowledgements

I would like to thank the following for providing helpful advice and information in the preparation phase of this book.

Nick Heasman
Hampshire Area Manager, South Downs National Park Committee, Queen Elizabeth Country Park, Gravel Hill, Horndean PO8 0QE.

Alison Perry
Footpaths and Access Officer, Hampshire County Council-Western Division, Queen Elizabeth Country Park, Gravel Hill, Horndean PO8 0QE.

Pamela Eastwood
Ranger, Forest of Bere, Forestry Commission, Forest Enterprise – South Downs Forest District Office, Bucks Horn Oak, Farnham GU10 4LS.

Introduction

This book contains the details of 20 walks in the Meon river valley area in southern Hampshire. The walks are suitable for novices, casual walkers, family groups, and experienced ramblers.

A river also rises ......

The river Meon is one of Hampshire's quintessential chalk streams. It rises from natural springs adjacent to South Farm in a bowl in the South Downs some twelve miles north of Portsmouth and just over a mile to the south of the village of East Meon. The river, which is impounded in a millpond immediately below its source, flows initially northwards and quickly gathers volume from two tributaries and additional springs on the lower slopes of Small Down. Within a mile of its source, it is a recognizable banked stream, two to four yards wide and eight to twelve inches deep on entering East Meon village where it flows between landscaped embankments.

Beyond the village the river turns in a north westerly direction through a more deeply etched and secluded valley for nearly three miles until West Meon. Beyond this village the river sweeps in a broad westerly arc to Warnford before turning south where its course, accompanied by the busy A32 main road between Fareham and Alton, occupies what is termed and known locally as the Meon Valley. The river retains the character of a clear, bubbling and picturesque stream past the villages of Exton, Meonstoke, Droxford, Soberton and the small town of Wickham to reach the outskirts of Fareham at Titchfield. For the remaining two and a half miles of its course, the river flows through water meadows and an internationally recognized bird and wildlife sanctuary to reach the Solent through estuarine marshes and a small man-made harbour at Hillhead. The length of the river from source to the sea is twenty–one miles.

A stream of surprises: a snapshot of the Meon in history

In length, width, depth and volume of water the Meon is not a mighty river. Through most of its course it appears placid and inconsequential. Yet it is also an idyllic watercourse neatly set into the rounded hills, wooded slopes, and the productive farmlands of southern England. Very nice to walk beside. Even nicer to sit by on one of the benches whilst drinking a pint of beer outside the Izaak Walton pub in East Meon on a warm, summer evening. A ripe subject for painters of landscapes. A nice stream to picnic by for an hour or so and then to move on to busier things. A good stream for a trout fisherman to cast a fly into.

Just like so many other rather taken-for-granted rivers such as the Eastern Rother in Sussex and the lower Frome in Dorset. Just one more quiet English stream hardly noticed by the busy motorist crossing the bridge at Titchfield in heavy rush-hour traffic on the A27. Pleasant enough, but what does it do? What is it for? Who lived and died by it? How did it get there? Why are parts of it so chocolate box pretty and the stuff of scenic postcards? Why is its valley such a delight to walk in and around? In what ways is it a mirror of the South Country in general?

Standing on the old Meon Valley railway embankment across the river from Droxford, and looking at the expanse of lush watermeadows framing the church tower of St Mary and All Saints, these are the sorts of questions that might come into the mind of the more than casual observer. A keen independent walker. A fly fisherman perhaps. A dairy farmer. A member of the Ramblers Association. A watercolourist. An ardent conservationist. The answers to such questions are quite profound. The river is the product of the complex geology and hydrology of the chalk and clay substructure below its bed. Its water clarity and the abundant fish and wildlife in it and on it is a function of the relative absence of domestic and industrial pollution and the purifying effects of the calcium in the chalk. Its meanders, banks, millraces, floodponds, watercress beds and canalized stretches are the product of man intervening and collaborating with nature over the centuries. The busy roads that follow it and the railway that once ran through its valley reflect the classic geographical principle of a routeway of least resistance. The settlements along its course drew and continue to draw drinking water from it. The growing of crops and the nurturing of livestock on its flatlands and downland slopes are made possible by its presence.

In Saxon times the Northumbrian bishop Wilfred preached to and converted the peoples of the Meon Valley. In the lower valley, the 18th century iron master Henry Cort perfected new smelting techniques in the Industrial Revolution. Where the Meon joins the sea at Hillhead, the 3rd Earl of Southampton used its waters to create one of the earliest navigable canals in Britain. In the upper valley the lands were once part of a royal demesne, the manorial properties of Alfred the Great. At Titchfield, a great Tudor palace was fashioned from the impressive ruins of a Premonstratensian abbey, complete with productive gardens and fishponds, to entertain kings and queens. At Droxford in a railway carriage on a siding of the Meon Valley line, Eisenhower and Churchill met in 1944 to discuss the plans for D Day and the liberation of Europe. In more recent times , notorious events in British post-World War II politics possibly concluded with the controversial repatriation of the mortal remains of Guy Burgess from Russia to a quiet cemetery in West Meon.

In the 20th century, trout hatcheries, timber millers, vineyards, garden centres, commercial watercress growers and even improbable alpaca and ostrich farms have found profitable locations close to the river. The valley and surrounding hills have played host to Jutes and Saxons, to Iron and Bronze Age dwellers of more than 1000 years BC, to Roman estate farmers following Vespasian's military domination of the area in AD79, and to the Norman invaders who wrote their rules for the ownership and usage of this landscape into their *Domesday Book.*

A small river then in physical appearance, but a surprisingly 'big' one in terms of the broad sweep of English history. A river with a story to tell, views to revere, secrets to reveal, reaches and bywaters to explore and wonderful footpaths to follow in and around one of the most picturesque valleys in Hampshire.

The South Downs – England's newest National Park

On the 12th November 2009 the Secretary of State for the Environment, Food and Rural Affairs signed the government edict bringing into legal existence the South Downs National Park. This culminated a long process by campaigners to give the unique chalk landscape of the South Downs protected status. The South Downs is the only national park in the British Isles to include full chalk landscapes. The headwater basin of the Meon river, and indeed much of its lower valley now lies within the designated boundary of the Western Section of the new national park.

For those who live within easy access to the chalk country of south-east England, the downland landscape with its pattern of gentle and open grassy slopes, cultivated river valleys, characteristic beechwoods, and picturesque nucleated villages often clustering around a church with a prominent tower or spire are known and often much-loved. To locals, the countryside is a pleasant commonplace, the scenic parts of which are within an hour's drive of large cities and towns such as Portsmouth, Worthing, Southampton and Brighton.

It is doubtful if the downland is the subject of much introspection or landscape appreciation to urban dwellers save for the members of the various societies that have a vested interest. Yet the geology and scenery of this region is geographically unique. Simply put, there is not a lot of chalk about! At least not on a world scale. Only northern France can boast a landscape that is structurally, if not scenically, the counterpart of the chalk downs of the south-east of England. There are but bits of chalk in Germany and Denmark. So a new national park for parts of downland Hampshire and much of Sussex is to be welcomed. The chalk is of national significance, part of heritage England, or 'White Cliffs consciousness' if you prefer.

There is a chance now that the landward encroachment of the suburbs of Portsmouth, Southampton, Worthing, Brighton and Eastbourne in particular will be controlled. This may be especially good news for the upper Meon basin which lies only three miles or so across Hyden Hill from Clanfield, which is essentially an urban settlement, previously called an 'overspill', of the city of Portsmouth. A planning framework for the careful conservation of the countryside means that the Meon river and its valley villages should retain in significant measure their ancient and scenic character. The South Downs National Park Authority though, is keen to develop a national park for the 21st Century.

It does not envisage an inert landscape pickled in aspic! A central aspiration is to encourage people to become proactive within the natural environment rather than just visit it and regard it from the car parks! Walking is a potentially crucial activity for the realization of this philosophy of involvement now being actively encouraged by the national parks movement.

What's in a name?

The name 'meon' is old, very old! Its origin and derivation can only be hinted at.

It may be a corruption of 'main' as in the River Main in Germany. This part of Hampshire is known to have been settled by ethnic Germans known to social historians as Jutes. It is possible they carried the name 'main' with them into the area. Folklore, eked out with references from the Anglo Saxon Chronicles to a series of incursions into the Isle of Wight, Hampshire and Kent in or about 495AD, refers to the incomers as the 'meonwarra' people. This group may have been ethnically distinct from the West Saxons, whose pattern of settlement, political organization and influence more visibly coalesced into the Kingdom of Wessex. Whatever its origin the term 'Meon' has survived both in the name of the river and valley that is the subject of this book, and as a description of the area of land several miles east and west of the river and taking in the coastal stretch of the Solent shore around Titchfield, Hillhead and Lee on Solent.

A fragment of geology

Like other Hampshire rivers, particularly the Itchen, Test and Hamble, the Meon is part of the complex hydrology and drainage of what is sometimes confusingly referred to as 'The Hampshire Basin'. This is a geological term, not much used outside earth science circles, to describe the underlying rock structure of Hampshire, the Isle of Wight, and parts of Dorset and Sussex. The northern boundary of the 'Basin' takes in the chalk uplands of the Salisbury Plain and the South Downs, and the lesser known area of Cranborne Chase. The southern boundary is marked by the strikingly visible ridge of the Purbeck Hills. This dips under the sea at Old Harry Rocks near Swanage. It emerges from the sea at the Needles and forms a continuous west-east spine through the Isle of Wight.

The basin extends for about 100 miles from Dorchester in the west to the cliffs of Beachy Head in the east. The chalk uplands, somewhat ironically called *downs* are the most striking surface feature of the Basin. They were formed in the relatively recent geological period of the Cretaceous age, between 145.4 and 65.5 million years ago. The chalk is a fine, soft white limestone made up from the calcareous remains of tiny sea creatures and plants. At one time the chalk formed a 'roof' over parts of Hampshire, Kent and Sussex. Under earth movements, erosion and a sustained if gradual rise in sea-level since the Quaternary Glaciation (or 'Last Great Ice Age' if you prefer), the 'roof' was eventually worn away to leave the classic scarp edges of the North and South Downs, exposing underlying strata of sands, clays and gravels. Some of these marine and freshwater deposits have come to have recognizably public names such as the 'Greensand Ridges' and the 'Gault Clay'.

Basins usually have to have something in them! In the case of the Hampshire Basin, it became filled with what are described as 'Tertiary Deposits', geologically young layers of sand, gravel, flints, brick-earth, clay and soils that filled the 'syncline' of the basin after the Cretaceous period had ended. It is over these Tertiary Deposits that the rivers of Hampshire run and upon which the villages and farms stand and historically depended. The conspicuous springs that emerge at the foot of the chalk scarps to feed rivers such as the Meon, indicate the line of separation between the porous chalk and the impervious clay. Along these 'lines of separation' people built houses, formed communities, farmed the lands, cut timber from the beech and oak woods that came to grow on the lower slopes and created a network of footpaths and trackways that have survived to this day. By this river people lived, worked, laughed, loved, and died! The original inhabitants may have been the 'Meonwarra'. Their latter-day successors are the people of Titchfield, Wickham, Soberton, Droxford, Meonstoke and West and East Meon. Through the varied walks that make up the rest of this book, there is an opportunity to encounter and know some details of life past and present in the downlands and in the discrete and unique settlements linked by the waters of the Meon River.

Walking in the South Country

Walking for pleasure and exercise in the south-eastern corner of England is generally delightful. There are no high mountains to climb. Nowhere does the high ground reach 1000 feet above sea level. There are no arduous and rocky mountain paths to negotiate as in the Pennines, Lake District, Snowdonia and the Scottish Highlands. What gradients there are, and some of the downland slopes can be steep, are not extended and usually managed without too much heavy breathing or physical discomfort. The ancient and extensive network of footpaths that criss-cross the region provide superb access to some of the most beautiful scenery and charming villages to be found anywhere in the United Kingdom. The climate in the south is blessed with generally warm summers and mild winters. The rivers that flow over the impervious clays in the valley bottoms may flood after heavy winter rain but such phenomena are not a serious impediment to country walking. All this means that the walker does not need expensive equipment or clothing.

In summer, indeed the lightest of clothes and simple footwear such as well-knitted socks and a good pair of trainers is all that is needed. However, most keen walkers wear good boots, a practice I would recommend. They should be waterproof but not very heavy. Walking in the south often involves following paths across ploughed fields. Soil accumulates on boots in such conditions quickly making them twice as heavy. Similarly, a light nylon waterproof jacket, easily folded and kept in a small rucksack is sufficient top-cover when the odd shower of rain occurs. Heavy anoraks and cagoules over a warm, wool sweater are only really needed in the depths of winter when the strong and prevailing south-westerly winds can make walking on the exposed ridgeline paths a potentially chilling experience.

Settlements are in close proximity in the south-east. Delightful old pubs and country tea rooms can be found almost everywhere. This means that carrying large supplies of food and drink is not necessary, unless you plan to have a country picnic. However, there is an exception to this general rule. If you walk the high and dry ridge lines of the downland you will usually have to descend to the valley to find refreshment. This can involve extra physical effort and a diversion from planned routes. So – it is always good to have something available to drink whilst out walking and a few light snacks and glucose-based, energy-producing sweets are also a good idea.

Established and long distance walking routes

A number of major gazetted routeways pass along and/or cross the Meon Valley. These routes are used in various combinations in the walks in this book. The most famous of these is the South Downs Way. It runs for more than 80 miles from Winchester in the west to end in the dramatic chalk cliff of Beachy Head above Eastbourne. Most of the time, the route progresses along the classic scarp ridge of the South Downs offering magnificent 360 degree views. Equally attractive but shorter is The Wayfarers Walk that starts at Emsworth on the coast and heads north to Inkpen Beacon in north Hampshire. Other named and waymarked routes are The Pilgrims Trail, The Monarch's Way, and The Lower Meon Valley Trail. Use is made in several walks of the trackbed of the former Meon Valley Railway (MVR) and the abandoned Botley-Bishops Waltham branch line. These are referred to in the book as the *railway paths.*

Hampshire County Council and the new South Downs National Park Authority have major responsibilities in respect of the stewardship and maintenance of these gazetted routes. Note that all the walks in this book are circular – starting and finishing at the same place. All of the walks can be fitted into a convenient five hour time frame, say between 10am and 3pm. Indeed, many can be comfortably fitted into a morning or an afternoon. Where appropriate, extensions to the walks to visit places and points of interest are included in the 'By the Way' section after the Walk Directions.

Public transport

The start point for most of the walks can be reached by public transport. The main points of departure are Fareham, Winchester, Bishops Waltham and Petersfield.

Fareham has a mainline railway station which can be used to access Walks 16 and 17. Walk 17 can also be accessed in less than 20 minutes using First Hampshire and Dorset circular bus services 6, 6A, 26 and 28 from Fareham Bus Station to Highlands Road shops.

Brijan Tours runs bus service 17 up much of the Meon valley. This service originates in Bishops Waltham and travels to Petersfield (for rail connection on the Portsmouth-London Waterloo line). Stops are made at Swanmore, Droxford, Corhampton, Warnford and West and East Meon. The service is regular but not frequent and does not operate on Sundays and Bank Holidays. Walks 2, 4, 5, 6, 7, 8, 9, 10, 12 and 18 can be accessed using this service.

First Hampshire and Dorset bus service 5A from Fareham go to Hill Head Road close to the start of Walks 19 and 20.

Stagecoach service 69 from Winchester to Fareham serves Wickham for Walks 14 and 15.

Advanced planning is required for walks using public transport. Given the variable nature of bus and train times, it is always best to check routes and timetables prior to setting out. See:

Brijan Tours
Tel: 01489 788338 **www.brijantours.com/busservices.htm**
First Hampshire and Dorset
Tel: 0870 010 6022 **www.firstgroup.com/firsthampshire**
Stagecoach
Tel: 0845 121 0190 **www.stagecoachbus.com/south**

Maps

Indicative sketch maps are provided for each walk. I do though, advise using this book in conjunction with one or more of the Ordnance Survey maps that cover the area. The Meon Valley is fortunate in being covered by two of the 1:25,000 (two and a half inches to one mile) Explorer Series. Much of the valley is covered by Sheet 119 Meon Valley – Portsmouth, Gosport and Fareham. The northern section of the valley is also covered by Sheet 132 Winchester, New Alresford and East Meon. The scale of these maps is particularly useful for walkers and the majority of footpaths and tracks are well-defined on these sheets.

Landranger Series Sheet 185 Winchester and Basingstoke covers most of the central and upper part of the valley from Soberton northwards. The lower section of the valley, from Wickham to the Solent seashore is covered by Landranger Sheet 196 The Solent and the Isle of Wight. For Butser Hill and the Queen Elizabeth Country park area of the South Downs, you need to refer to Landranger Sheet 197 Chichester and the Downs. All three Landranger maps are at the scale of 1:50,000 or one and a quarter inches to one mile if you prefer.

The Countryside Code

For many years walkers and other users of the countryside have been asked to respect and to follow The Countryside Code. This is really a commonsense charter. In summary the code asks walkers to:

- plan ahead for safe and sensible walking
- obey and follow signs and warnings as encountered
- leave gates and property as you find them
- avoid damaging plants and animals and do not pick wildflowers
- keep dogs under close control especially near livestock
- kespect other people especially those who live and work in the country

The code is under the stewardship of Natural England. The revised (2004) edition of the code elaborates in detail on the above key points, outlines a code for land managers, and has useful additional sections on rights and responsibilities and regional directories for places to visit and sites in the natural environment of special scientific interest. Several of such places are incorporated into walks in this book. See **www.naturalengland.org.uk**

Child friendly walking

Many of the walks in this book can be successfully undertaken by physically healthy children over the age of about seven. However, the walks of eight miles or more are probably best reserved for the over-11s. Walking with children in the countryside can be the most delightfully rewarding experience for parents and adults. It can be wonderful to see the smile of delight on a young child's face as she or he spots for the very first time say, a squirrel busily gathering nuts, or a woodpecker busily hammering out a hole in a tree. The countryside is a wonderful teacher for children. However, you do need to know the moods and capacities of your children! They can easily expend their day's ration of energy in the first fifteen minutes of a walk, charging backwards and forwards along the bank of a river, playing hide and seek in the woods, climbing trees and so on. This can leave children, not to mention parents, fractious and exhausted with, perhaps, still several miles of a walk to go. Similarly, children have a limited capacity to take in information about landscape and scenery, no matter how well-intentioned the 'instruction' might be by adults. What interests an adult does not necessarily interest a child. However, children are curious and will be motivated and delighted by surprises along the way. A function of good route planning is to know where these surprises are. An attractive footbridge over a millstream, a couple of alpacas in a field, the bole of an old oak with the face of a figure carved into it (plus the story that goes with it). All these can be found to make walking with children a 'discovery' and an adventure.

Also, and without impinging too much on child freedom, a few basic ground rules and practices, mostly commonsense, need to be adhered to. These include the wearing of correctly laced footwear with non-slip soles, staying in sight of the footpath and adults, not getting too far ahead or behind, always waiting at stiles and river crossing places and so on. Particular care has to be taken in supervising children when walking along roads where traffic is likely. The usual practice here is to walk on the verge facing oncoming traffic, in a close single file, one adult at the front, one adult at the rear, and the children in-between. Children usually like, if they don't exactly need, regular sustenance. Diluted orange and lemon juice make good drinks. Fizzy drinks in ring-pull cans are to be avoided. Snacks such as a variety of fruits and cheese fingers and carrot and celery 'stickmen' can also keep children going whilst dangling the idea of a full picnic in some delightful spot a mile or two down the pathway.

Finally, it is useful for one adult to carry a small First Aid kit. This should contain a range of plasters, antiseptic and insect bite cream, and a reasonably sized bandage for the almost inevitable scrapes, blisters, minor cuts and abrasions that seem to follow children around the countryside. Most importantly, walking in the countryside should be a happy and pleasant experience for everyone. Keep up a regular pace but avoid over-exertion. You should stop briefly about every fifteen minutes to take in the view and to listen for the sound of farm animals and birds. If you can do these simple things you may be a bit physically tired at the end of your walk – but you will be also invigorated and thoroughly delighted with your endeavours and achievements!

1: Over the 'Roof' of Hampshire
The Traverse of Butser Hill

Highest point in Hampshire – Airy and open downland – Long views to the sea

Distance	5.5 miles
Approximate time	Two and a half hours
Start and finish	The Visitor Centre car park at the Queen Elizabeth Country Park, on the A3. 14 miles north of Portsmouth. 4 miles south of Petersfield. Grid reference 718185
Refreshments	The Visitor Centre has a café, shop and toilets
Map	OS 1:50,000 Landranger Sheet 197 Chichester

Butser Hill at 886 feet above sea level feet is the highest point in Hampshire. The hill has an extensive, grassy, plateau-like summit area crowned by a very conspicuous communications tower, a landmark for miles around. The hill rises above and effectively encloses the Meon valley on the west. To the east, the classic scarp of the South Downs rolls off into Sussex to terminate at Beachy Head. The summit area has a popular 'top' car park, seasonally-opening cafe and picnic area. There are numerous walking paths. Much frequented at any time of year, walking, bird-watching, kite flying and BMX riding are some of the activities that go on up here. Many people are content to simply walk up to the summit and back to the Visitor Centre. A pleasant two and a half mile stroll or so for some of the finest views in the south of England. The walk listed here is a genuine 'there and back' hike taking you right up and over Butser and down the other side into the Meon Valley. Thus you will ascend the hill twice involving rather more than 1500 feet of vertical ascent. However, the distance is not great, the ascents are gradual, and the walk is not arduous. Indeed, on the second ascent from the Meon Valley, altitude is regained almost without noticing. The descents are a delight providing long vistas over the 'roof' of Hampshire. To the purists of the hill-walking fraternity, Butser is a 'Marilyn', that is an English hill over 492 feet in height, one of an identified 1555 such eminences in the United Kingdom. The term 'Marilyn' is an ironic reposte to the designation of Scottish mountains as 'Monroes', that is, mountains over 3000 feet high.

1. **From the Visitor Centre car park, walk back along the approach road under the A3. Cross the approach road at the first fingerpost signed 'South Downs Way'. Cross the overflow car park and in a few yards go right at the blue acorn sign and pass through the gate.**

The route ahead is now unmistakeable. You simply climb the broad, grassy, central spur of Butser direct to the communications

Butser Hill at 886 feet above sea level is the highest point in Hampshire and a popular beauty spot

tower at the top. This takes about 25 minutes and, in geographical terms, you are actually ascending the 'dip slope' of the South Downs escarpment. You will pass through another 'acorn gate' about two thirds of the way up.

2. **As you approach the top, veer right towards the communications tower. Pass it on your left and progress to the trig column at the highest point on Butser.**

Pause and take in the wonderful prospect of the Downs rolling east, and the coast to the south. A fabulous place!

3. **With your back to the trig column, walk due west along the turf path for about two hundred yards. As the whole of the upper Meon valley opens out in front of you, turn right to pass a small fenced enclosure. Swing left to the stile by the bushes. Cross this stile and keep ahead now beginning to descend.**

Petersfield can be seen in the valley away down to your right.

Pass between gorse bushes and commence the steeper descent of this western shoulder of Butser.

Note the deep coombe of Rake Bottom falling away on your left. You will be surprised by how quickly you descend this open, western shoulder of Butser.

In a matter of minutes you will arrive at the trees where the path 'defiles' down to a gate.

4. **Cross the stile here and turn right onto the broad, rutted track that soon levels out. Reach a metalled lane and go left with the sign reading 'Oxenbourne'.**

You are now down on the floor of the Meon Valley proper.

5. **Walk for a couple of hundred yards along this lane with care as it has steep banks and no verge in the centre section. Just beyond the buttressed brick garden wall of Leythe House, turn left into the lane at the sign 'Except for Access'.**

Pass the cottage on the left and recommence the climb of Butser Hill at the short wooden posts, the left-hand one carrying a blue 'Off Road Cycle Trail' waymark. This is actually Limekiln Lane. This rough track now climbs up through the trees at an easy gradient.

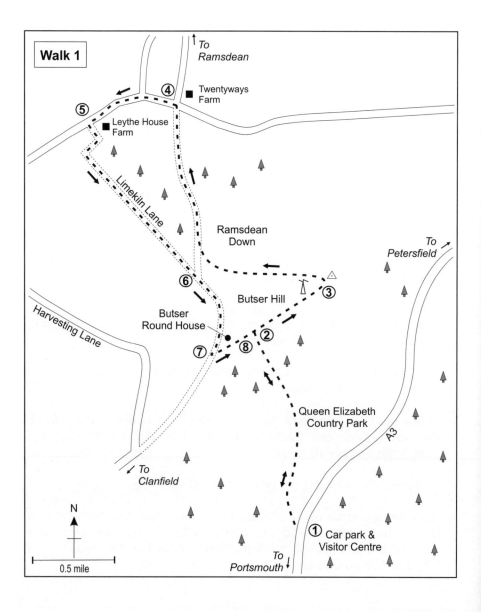

As it emerges from the trees along the lower spur, you can see the Butser Roundhouse cafe on the skyline ahead and slightly right. The bulk of the western slopes of Butser Hill now loom large ahead of you.

6. **The track converges at a stile with another path coming up from Rake Bottom to your left. Keep ahead and climb the flank of Butser Hill.**

Half way up this section, you will gain a magnificent view of the upper Meon valley. The spire of East Meon church can be seen in the distance to the right. The source springs of the Meon river are at South Farm in the middle ground of the valley below.

7. **When you reach the metalled lane at the top, turn acutely left at the 'South Downs Way Bridleway' sign and walk on the grass up to the Butser Roundhouse.**

8. **Just beyond the Roundhouse go through the gate and turn right at the fingerpost 'Visitor Centre via South Downs Way 2 km'.**

The Meon valley begins as a broad basin some three miles square

You now have a very pleasant downhill stroll to reach the visitor centre in about twenty minutes.

By the Way

The Queen Elizabeth Country Park at 600 hectares is one of largest and most popular country parks in Hampshire. It provides an ideal introduction to the South Downs. There are some 20 miles of hiking, cycling and horse-riding trails through mixed forests and over open downland. The park is an important habitat for English mammals, birds and 38 recorded species of butterfly and 12 recorded species of wild orchid.

A curious alpaca by the source of the Meon

There are facilities for children including adventure playgrounds and play areas for toddlers. Many public participation events are held in the park throughout the year. These include egg rolling down the hills at Easter, autojumble sales, assorted kite and model aeroplane flying meets, monthly exhibitions of artworks, and traditional agricultural, produce and crafts shows that take place in summer. The Coach House Café at the Visitor Centre makes a feature of using Hampshire produced foods in its daily menus. Also at the Visitor Centre is a small theatre and wildlife interpretation exhibition. There is a very well-stocked shop that retails many locally crafted items and a range of products focusing on natural environment themes.
Tel: 02392 595040 **www.hants.gov.uk/countryside/qecp**

2: A walk through the village of East Meon and on to the Downs

Picturesque village – Secluded woods and downs – Riverside paths

Distance	4 miles
Approximate time	Two hours and fifteen minutes
Start and finish	The free car park by the village green at the end of Workhouse Lane in East Meon. This village is 4.4 miles west of Petersfield. A good approach road is via Clanfield off the A3(M) north of Portsmouth. Grid reference 678223
Refreshments	East Meon has two well-known public houses, The George Inn and the Izaak Walton both situated in the centre of the village and both serve food. There is a village convenience store in the extension of the High Street
Map	OS 1:25,000 Explorer Sheet Winchester

This is a fairly short walk through the picturesque village of East Meon. The walk ascends to open downs, passes through some woodlands, and comes back downhill into the Meon river valley. No major difficulties are presented. The climb up Park Hill, behind the church is steep, but quickly accomplished and the view from the top is worth the effort. The walk makes use of broad footpaths and byways that are generally clearly signposted. In the later section, alongside Greenway Copse, the track is boggy in winter when water is siphoned off from the drainage channels and raised fields hereabouts.

1. **Walk along Workhouse Lane with its pretty thatched cottages and timber framed buildings towards the centre of the ancient Domesday village of East Meon.**

   Turn left into The Cross to see the original course of the Meon. In its former course, the river had the habit of flooding the village after heavy rain. You can see the flood mitigation features of the newer, straightened channel of the Meon here also.

2. **Retrace your steps to Workhouse Lane and then turn left up Church Street to All Saints church.**

   Note the old village well and plaque in the garden of the historically significant Forbes Almshouses. Take some time to visit the interior of the attractive and much-photographed Norman church. Note the black marble baptismal font from Tournai. Another treasure on display is the Millennium Tapestry showing scenes of daily life in this picturesque village.

3. **From the Lych Gate, take the path up through the churchyard to the left to the '18 steps' in the top corner before the stile. Cross this and turn half-right to ascend some 330 feet to the crest of Park Hill.**

   This is a wonderful spot and the short if steep climb rewards you with some of the finest downland views in Hampshire. The church and the village are tucked neatly into the hillside below. The whole of the headwater basin of the Meon river spreads before you. Butser Hill, dominates the scene two miles to the south east. From the northern shoulder of Butser, the South Downs take on their characteristic, scarp-like appearance and roll eastwards into Sussex. Due south across the Meon Valley, and above the springs at South Farm that are the source of the river, the radio masts of the former Royal Navy Communcations School of HMS Mercury still stand on top of Wether Down. To the west the Meon River valley closes in below the slopes of Hen Wood.

4. **At the crest of Park Hill, turn right to follow the fence line above Vineyard Hole and follow the track as it swings north alongside the fence above a pleasant side valley.**
   With Park Cottage in view, cross a stile and veer right across the field to a further stile. Cross it and go ahead parallel to the sunken

The much-loved Church of All Saints at East Meon, tucked in under the steep slope of Park Hill

lane on the right. At the end of the small field, at Park Farm, cross the stile and effectively turn right across the lane.

5. Enter the field at the 'footpath' signed fingerpost and continue up the slope on the broad farm track. Go along the left edge of the field. At the next fingerpost – by the pine plantation – go right, and in 50 yards left.

You are now faced with one of my favourite hidden valleys high up amongst the Downs. The area is a gentle landscape of open hillside, broad leaf woodland, and hidden coombes. It is an area that is little visited but is none the less delightful for that. There are pleasant spots here and around the shoulder of Scaffolds Row for a drink or a picnic or a spot of birdwatching.

6. Descend to the clearly visible fingerpost at the bottom of the hollow, which is signed 'bridleway'. Turn right here, and still on a broad

track walk ahead to the trees. At the junction in front of the trees go left and immediately loop down right into the wood.

This surprisingly sharp descent of the coombe between Rookham Copse and Sir Williams Hill is accompanied with a wonderful prospect of Butser Hill as you clear the trees.

7. At the foot of the hill leave the broad track , which veers off to the right. Instead, keep ahead along the left side of the field still signed 'bridleway'. This partly sunken route shortly leads you to a gate by a house. Cross the East Meon to Langrish minor road with care and go right along the verge (there is a blind bend in the road ahead which you need to be mindful of) for 100 yards.

8. Veer left at the orange 'byway' signpost. Go ahead along this broad byway, which offers very well-established examples of coppicing in its borders.

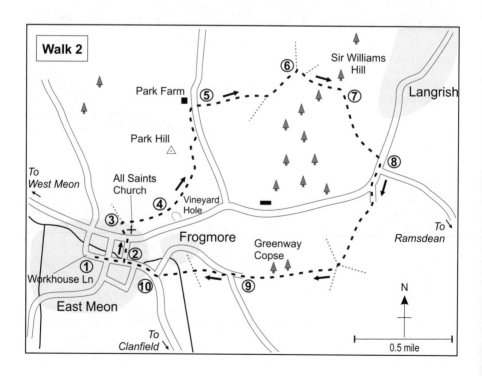

At the major 'fiveways' track junction in a clearing, turn right. There is no signpost here for the direction you want to follow but the route is westerly and fairly obvious. You need to avoid taking the track that goes acutely off to the right. Pass Greenway Copse on the right and beyond the metal gate, join a house access track. This tree-canopied way in turn leads to a metalled lane.

9. Cross to the fingerpost signed 'footpath' and cross the stile. Cross the field ahead slightly left of centre to the next stile. Cross this and also immediately the one on the right. With the river now next to you on the left, go through three gates in quick succession to join the road at Frogmore.
   Turn left along the road for a few yards to the brick and flint bridge over the Meon.

Pause a while here to admire the traditionally thatched cottages and outbuildings clustering by the bridge. A very photogenic place.

10. Now take the very pleasing bitumenised path that hugs the right bank of the river to pass in front of cottages and the East Meon village allotments on the left.
    Re-enter the village through the 'tunnel' between the thatched cottages.

You come out right beside The Izaak Walton pub. Perhaps you might like to take some refreshment here before you commence your homeward journey!

By the Way

East Meon is in many ways a classic English nucleated village with a very long settlement history. A history that in some measure recalls the history of England itself. A cluster of old cottages and inns at a bridging point over the Meon, overlooked by an imposing church on the side of Park Hill, give it that timeless quality characteristic of many rural settlements in the south of England. Burial barrows in the parish, the Iron Age fort on Old Winchester Hill, and vestigial Roman remains, all provide testimony to the long-settled and farmed character of the upper Meon Valley. Later incorporation into the Royal Saxon manors of Alfred the Great and fragmentary references to land grants by King Edgar for the building of a

The river runs through it – the infant Meon beside the High St in East Meon

church point to the antiquity of East Meon. The Normans came this way of course, post 1066. The village is mentioned in William the Conqueror's *Domesday Book* and the imposing bulk of All Saints Church is a powerful expression of Norman ecclesiastical architecture. From the Middle Ages, social life in East Meon came under the influence (some historians say 'control') of the politically and religiously powerful Bishops of Winchester. The Court House with its medieval hall near the church dates from this period. Later still during the English Civil War, the Parliamentary forces prepared for the Battle of Cheriton (1644) from encampments round and about East Meon. Some village histories report that the soldiers stole lead from the church font to make bullets! Probably an apocryphal story – but who really knows?

In the 21st century East Meon like all English villages, has had to accommodate public housing and new residential developments within its boundaries. However, the village retains its charm as the centerpiece settlement in the upper Meon.

An acknowledgement of the place of East Meon in English history took place in 1986.

During that year, the 900th anniversary of *Domesday Book*, East Meon was selected as 'The Domesday Village'. A model of the village as it might have looked in 1086 was constructed and exhibited in the Great Hall in Winchester. The model is now, apparently, co-located with the Bayeux Tapestry in Normandy.

3: By hidden lakes and along airy ridges to find Mercury on Wether Down

South Downs Way – Hidden lakes – HMS Mercury

Distance	7.5 miles
Approximate time	Three and a half hours
Start and finish	At the Old Winchester Hill National Nature Reserve car park and picnic grounds. This is reached via a sporty, single carriageway (with passing places) metalled lane that leaves the A32 at Warnford, almost opposite the George and Falcon public house. Grid reference 645215
Refreshments	Carry some refreshments with you, particularly something to drink.The George and Falcon in Warnford can be visited at the end of the walk. There is also a lodge at Meon Springs Fly Fishery that offers refreshments on active fishing days
Map	OS 1:25,000 Explorer Sheet Winchester

This is a superb, rather energetic 'down and up' walk that provides magnificent views throughout. The Coombe valley, which is descended into at the start of the walk, is a scenic delight. Enclosed by Old Winchester Hill on the west and the extensively wooded slopes of Henwood Down on the east, the valley contains springs and a stream that broadens out into two popular fishing lakes, Whitewool and Coombe. The outflow from these becomes a tributary of the Meon reaching the main channel of the river at East End. There is long, gradual ascent up the ridge of Salt Hill to reach the landmark communications masts of the former Royal Navy establishment of HMS Mercury high on Wether Down. Later, there is a short but quite steep climb up the north-eastern side of Teglease Down back to the start point.

1. **Turn left out of the car park back along the road for about 275 yards to the fork. A path by the fence on the right facilitates progress. Enter the gate on the right by the sign 'South Downs Way. Public Bridleway'.**

   Angle right on the broad, grassy track down the field with Whitewool Farm in view in the valley below. At the chalk-pit at the base of the scarp, turn left at the 'South Downs Way Bridleway' fingerpost and approach the farm buildings. Go to the left of these still following the bridleway to reach the Meon Springs fishery complex.

As you cross the bridge between Coombe and Whitewool Lakes, pause to admire the attractive weirs and landscaped waters. On the Whitewool Lake side, just to the left, there is an attractively-styled timber fishing lodge that may be open for refreshments (see 'By Your Way' at the end of the walk directions).

The South Downs Way approaches Whitewool Farm

2. **Go up to the lane and turn right. Walk along it to pass Hall Cottage on the left. Just beyond, turn left at the 'South Downs Way Bridleway' sign.**

 Follow the concrete farm track straight up the slope to pass through a gap in the trees. At the end of the second field, in the dip by the 'fourways' fingerpost, turn right. The direction you follow is signed 'South Downs Way. Public Bridleway. Butser Hill 4.5 miles'. You now commence the mile or so climb up the ridge of Salt Hill. On route, cross the lane by the properties at Coombe Cross and keep on going straight ahead towards the communication masts on Wether Down.

When you reach the masts, stop to do a full three hundred and sixty degree turn to take in the breathtaking views. It is quite obvious why the Royal Navy located its communications training facility here: seclusion, security and uninterrupted air waves and lines of sight to the dockyard in Portsmouth. Note the trig column built right on top of the grassed-over concrete bunker adjacent to the masts.

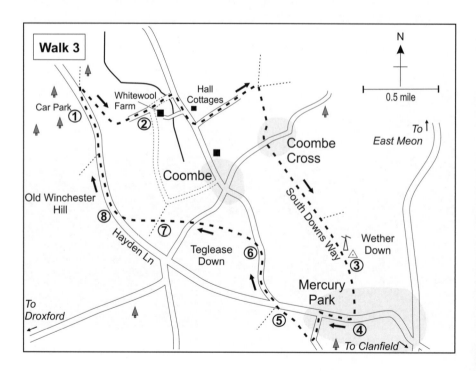

Whitewool Lake, an attractive and popular trout fishery

3. **Continue past the masts down to the road to the point where the abandoned buildings of HMS Mercury now sit somewhat forlornly behind the razor wire.**

   Opposite, on a developed part of the site, is the Wether Down Hostel and Sustainability Centre. This hosts parties of schoolchildren and others for courses in woodcraft, nature studies and sustainable rural lifestyles. The site also incorporates a natural woodland burial site.

4. **Turn right along the road here to pass Leydene Garden Farms on the left. In a further 150 yards turn left onto the farm track. At the open sided barn turn right at the 'Restricted Byway' sign.**

   There are excellent views to the south from this pleasant byway.

5. **At the road cross to the sign 'Meon Springs Fly Fishery'. Follow the metalled lane as it descends quite steeply toward Coombe. After about 6-8 minutes walking, where the lane levels out and the valley**

ahead opens up, leave the lane through the gate at the fingerpost on the left. The path now contours around and below the bulk of Teglease Down. Go through a gate to a lane.

6. Turn left up the lane for just a few yards to go through another gate at the fingerpost on the right. In 20 yards cross another stile signed 'The Monarch's Way'.

You are now confronted by a large and undulating field. It may be heavily cultivated in summer and the path across it indistinct.

Follow the direction indicated by the finger post but please do avoid trampling any crops that might be growing here. The route initially swings left across the field and then curves right towards the edge of the nearer woodland on the skyline.

As you cross the central undulations of this field, the initially hidden Castle Cottages appear to your right.

The communication masts of HMS Mercury high on Wether Down

7. You will see the waymarked exit gate from the field about 250 yards to the left of these cottages. Take this and climb very steeply upwards to cross the stile into the recently planted woodland. Pass through the wood up to the road which you access over two stiles.

8. Turn right here and walk along the grassy, right-hand verge until you see the gate on the left leading into the Old Winchester Hill National Nature Reserve. Cross the road, go through the gate and go right to follow the 'South Downs Way' signed path parallel to the road (slightly longer than expected) to bring you back in due course to the car park.

By the Way
For details of lodge opening and fishing arrangements go to: www.meonsprings.co.uk

HMS Mercury
Royal Navy shore establishment, HMS Mercury was commissioned at Leydene House on the slopes of Wether Down on 16 August 1941. The training for radio operators and signallers which had taken place at several sites and HM Barracks in Portsmouth since 1904, were eventually concentrated at this picturesque but rather remote site. The relatively high altitude, lack of radio clutter and interference often experienced in an urban area, plus the reduction of the possibility of bomb attacks from enemy air forces, meant training could continue uninterrupted. HMS Mercury eventually incorporated the communications and navigation facilities of the School of Maritime Operations of the Royal Navy. Fondly remembered by the generations of RN signallers and radio operators who trained here, HMS Mercury decommissioned on 31 August 1993.

Part of the site has been developed but the future of remaining buildings remains unclear.

4: A fleeting encounter with a hero and a villain on a walk starting in West Meon

Historic monuments – Picturesque farms – Famous and infamous people

Distance	7.8 miles
Approximate time	Four hours
Start and finish	The walk starts at the Thomas Lord public house in West Meon. The main village car park is at the top, right-hand end of Headon View adjacent to the hall and recreation ground. This is reached by turning left off the A32, just north of the village centre. Grid reference 643241
Refreshments	Thomas Lord and Red Lion pubs in West Meon. The Post Office and village stores incorporate a pleasant café
Map	OS 1:25,000 Explorer Sheet Winchester

This is a longer and reasonably strenuous walk 'touching' many aspects of the social and economic history of the area. It involves the use of less frequented paths and bridleways in the secluded high ground to the north of the upper section of the Meon Valley. The paddocks, cultivated 'hollow' fields, woodlands and picturesque farms neatly embedded into the landscape of this area often escape the attentions of casual walkers and visitors who tend to keep to the more public paths around the villages lower down by the river. If you want to be alone in your walking you are likely to be so on this route. The undulations in the landscape around Privett in particular mean that this walk provides what the rambling fraternity calls a 'good stretch into the backblocks'. The physical effort is well worth making. There are some stunningly beautiful pockets of country in this secluded part of Hampshire.

1. **With your back to the Thomas Lord pub go left along the road towards East Meon. Walk on the pavement on the right alongside the overflow channel of the Meon river.**

   Note the ivy-covered concrete blocks and ironwork up to the right as you pass through the gap that was once spanned by a mighty 62 foot high steel railway viaduct. These are all that remain of the structure dismantled for scrap in 1956. Should you wish to visit the parish Church of St John the Evangelist and the tombs in the churchyard at the end of the walk, a delightful village path starts just before the viaduct site here. It crosses the river and winds round the back of the village to cross the A32 and then goes up to the churchyard. This takes five minutes or so and is a nice alternative to the walk along the road from the pub to the church.

2. **A short distance past the viaduct site and at the bus stop hard by the river, cross the road to the pavement on the other side and walk on to quickly reach East End. Turn left into Vinnells Lane and in 50 yards turn right onto the footpath. This winds around the backs of ornate gardens. Cross a stile and walk up the field keeping to the left edge.**

   Look to your right for a 'spot shot' of the communications tower on Butser Hill to the east.

   Cross the next stile and go half-right to another one. Cross this also and follow the right-hand edge of the field to the next stile in the top right corner. The waymark here points straight ahead across a curious 'hollow' field that may well have a crop growing in it. Cross the field and ascend a grassy bank to exit the field to a metalled lane through a gap in the hedgerow.

3. **Turn right down this tree-lined lane.**

   Note the curious cricket pavilion on the right. When you reach the main road to East Meon, cross to the verge in front of the restored Westbury House, a once stately Palladian manor that dominates the upper Meon

Valley. To the right just in the trees, is the ruin of the Chapel of St Nicholas, a scheduled ancient monument predating the Norman Conquest. The river here passes through the grounds and is impounded to form an ornamental lake. The house endured a catastrophic fire in 1904 during which the then owner, a Colonel Le Roy Lewis, who had won a DSO in the Boer War, engaged in further gallantry by saving his five children and their governesses from the flames. Rebuilt by this gentleman-of-means but auctioned as a complete farm estate in 1918, the house and lands eventually became

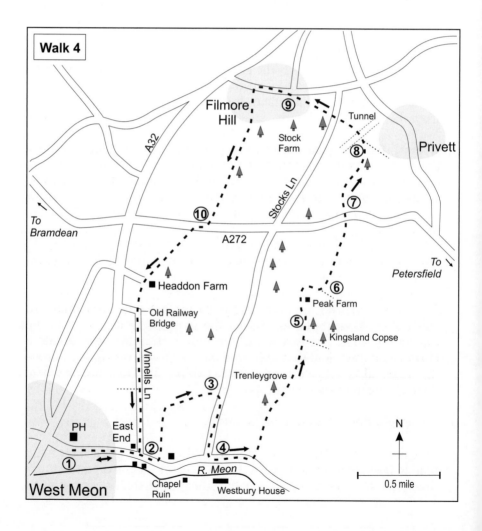

separated. The house came to serve many purposes down the years. It remained a school for a long time. During World War II, works of art and nationally important museum pieces were brought here from London for safekeeping. Note the superbly converted stable block. Westbury House is currently a nursing home.

4. Walk along the right verge of the main road in an easterly direction for 275 yards towards East Meon. Where the road bends cross with care to the signpost opposite. Now follow the indicated route in a northerly direction, gradually ascending and keeping to the left side of fields.

In the vicinity of Trenleygrove Plantation on the left, pause and look around. This is one of the most beautiful parts of the Meon Valley.

As you reach the top of this long pull, go through the gate and approach Peak Farm over stiles with the woodland of Kingsland Copse now on the right. From the edge of this copse, ascend the sloping field to the left to a fingerpost at a 6-bar metal gate.

5. Go ahead down the track with the buildings of Peak Farm now on your immediate right. The track joins a metalled lane just by the farm entrance gate. About 100 yards along this lane there is a 'byway' signpost on the right. Do not cross the stile in front of you. Instead, follow the byway indicator to go to the right through the gate. Then progress down the left-side of the field for about 50 yards.

6. Turn left through the gate with the yellow waymark. The route is now ahead through several gates and over fields with the landmark of Privett church spire on the skyline to guide you.

There may well be livestock in these fields. If so, it is important not to disturb them by irregular movements. Do please ensure all gates are closed behind you as you pass through these extensive farmlands. The gates and posts are typically waymarked but as you drop down towards the A272, the route tends to occupy the 'hollow' in the centre of the fields.

7. Cross the busy A272 with care and go right for a few yards to the fingerpost in the hedge. Follow in the direction indicated but at the

top of the first field angle right, and wind around the edge of the large second field up to the top right hand corner to converge with the cutting of the Meon Valley railway. Cross over the top of the portal of the long-closed Privett tunnel.

8. Turn left at the waymarked stile just beyond, and in 100 yards go left at the partially hidden waymark onto a fenced path.

   You will see Stock Farm down to your left. At the end of the fenced path cross a stile to a track. Turn right and almost immediately left at the fingerpost. Follow the path through Lime Copse to emerge at the edge of a large field. Cross this field by veering right towards a conspicuous circular yellow waymark just to the left of the garden of the 'white house'. On reaching it be prepared for a small shock! You have to pass through a gate and across the side, manicured lawn of the house.

This happens more often than you might think in Hampshire. Anyway, do not be shy, cross the lawn in direct line as indicated to the 'lift' stile in the corner.

9. **Cross it and turn left along the lane until you reach the red post box on the right. Just beyond it, at Filmore Hill barn, turn left at the fingerpost signed 'bridleway'.**

See if you can visualize the 'ram's head' sculpture in the dead tree here.

Go straight down the bridleway to the A272, which you cross once more.

On your way down look for the Meon Hut, a popular bikers and car rally roadhouse, in the valley to the lower right.

10. **After crossing the A272, go right along the verge for about 75 yards. Turn left onto the unsigned trackway between two metal gates.**

This 'unadopted road' is a shaded and tree-lined routeway. It is soft underfoot and pleasant to walk along.

At Headdon Farm buildings keep straight ahead and then shortly turn left over an old brick railway bridge. Once crossed, veer right

to join the upper section of Vinnells Lane. This rises slowly to a crest where you gain yet another fine view over the upper Meon Valley. The lane then drops gradually down to East End where you turn right to return to return to the Thomas Lord pub.

By the Way

Privett Tunnel

At 1056 yards, this was the longest of the three tunnels on the Meon Valley Railway (MVR). In 1899 it was the scene of a tragedy during construction. Engineering techniques employed included the sinking of vertical access tunnels to the main horizontal line of the running tunnel far below. Men, equipment and even horses were lowered down these shafts to the workface. On the 27th of January, the sides of one of these shafts caved in trapping two workmen, James Owen and George Brown. Brown did not survive but Owen was rescued alive after two days and nights. Apparently cross-timbers had jammed above his head giving him just enough airspace and protection from the falling soil.

Brown poignantly recalled Owen's recitation of the *Lord's Prayer* and attempts to verbally pass details of his sister as next of kin prior to his realization of his fate. His body was recovered the following week.

In latter years the tunnels of the MV have been used for mushroom growing and the storage of scrap military hardware. Colonies of bats frequent the tunnels.

West Meon

This is an attractive village with thatched cottages and a large much-chimneyed manor house. It also has a fine 19th century church, St John the Evangelist, styled by the noted architect George Gilbert Scott in 'Revival' English Gothic style. The parish is believed to have had its origins during the missionary preaching of St Wilfred, an exiled Northumbrian bishop, active throughout the Meon Valley in the period 681-686 AD. In the churchyard are several graves of the great, the good, and the very-definitely not-so-good.

Thomas Lord (1755-1832)

Lord was a landowner and professional cricketer for the White Conduit Club in the area of London we now refer to as St John's Wood. He gave his name to Lord's, the ground that is forever the shrine of cricket.

As a bowler of some repute, he became strongly associated with

Middlesex cricket and the fortunes of the Marylebone Cricket Club (MCC). Under the influence and patronage of the Earl of Winchilsea and the Duke of Richmond, both reportedly 'cricket mad' aristocrats, Lord acquired seven acres in the Dorset Square part of London. This became the early home to the White Conduit Club, later to become the MCC. Lord later acquired 80 year leases on the Brick and Great Fields in St John's Wood. This became known as 'Lord's Middle Ground'. A further relocation to the present site of Lord's Cricket Ground was

The 'table' tomb of Thomas Lord (1755-1832) in the churchyard at West Meon. He gave his name to Lord's Cricket Ground in London

occasioned by the construction of the Regent's Canal and railway works. Lord was tempted to sell part of this land for housing to refill his rapidly emptying personal coffers! He was diverted from doing so by being bought out for £5000 by William Ward, also a keen cricketer, MCC Member and a Director of the Bank of England. The rest as they say is 'cricketing history'! Lord came to West Meon in 1830 to retire as a gentleman farmer. His very visible 'table' tomb in the churchyard is maintained to this day by MCC.

Guy Francis de Moncy Burgess (1911-1963)

More commonly known as Guy Burgess, it is both sad and ironic that one of the most notorious British spies and traitors of the twentieth century, should end up in an archetypal country churchyard deep in the beating heart of the country he betrayed.

Burgess, along with Kim Philby and Donald MacLean was part of the 'Cambridge Five' spy ring* that passed official military, government and MI5 secrets to the Soviet Union during the most serious days of the Cold War in the 1940s and 1950s. Burgess' position as secretary to the Foreign Secretary, Hector McNeil, gave him access to classified information which he passed to Russian controllers.

Later, during an assignment at the British Embassy in Washington DC, indiscreet homosexual behaviour and heavy drinking brought Burgess to the notice of the CIA and official suspicion of his activities was raised

Apparently about to be unmasked, he was warned beforehand by Kim Philby. Burgess and MacLean quickly disappeared through a 'pipeline' via Southampton organized by their Russian masters. They both arrived in Moscow in 1951 but this was not publicly confirmed until the pair were outed at a press conference in 1956. Maclean eventually became a Russian citizen and lived as a political exile in that country until his death in 1983. Philby also fled the west years after the original defections when it became his turn to fall under suspicion.

Burgess did not adjust to life in the Soviet Union and died there, alcoholic, unloved and alone in 1963 aged 52. At the request of his mother, his ashes were returned to the UK in the keeping of Burgess' brother who had attended the cremation in Moscow. Reports suggest the ashes were contained in an earthenware vessel adorned with Russian characters. The urn and/or its contents was buried in the dead of night and unpublicized for obvious reasons in a family plot in West Meon churchyard on 5th October 1963. There is no mention by name of Burgess in the history leaflet for Saint John the Evangelist. In respect of burials in the churchyard, there is a passing reference to a 'notorious' one. This may or may not refer to Burgess and the grave site to the north of the church tower has now, apparently, had identifying script removed from it.

* Kim Philby. Guy Burgess. Donald MacLean. Anthony Blunt. John Cairncross.

5: From watercress beds to a stately home: Warnford to Hinton Ampner

Watercress beds – Stately home and parkland – Open fields

Distance	8 miles
Approximate time	Four hours
Start and finish	Warnford Village Hall in Lippen Lane at Warnford on the A32. There is verge parking along Lippen Lane next to the childrens playground. Grid reference 624233
Refreshments	The George and Falcon pub in Warnford. Note that Kilmeston village at the half-way point has no shops or other facilities. The house at Hinton Ampner has a tea room serving light refreshments
Map	OS 1:25,000 Explorer Sheet Winchester

A longish, downland and farmland walk through some lovely countryside to Hinton Ampner, one of Hampshire's finest stately homes and landscaped gardens. The walk involves crossing some of the largest cultivated fields to be found anywhere. It is important to walk the gazetted paths across these fields to keep the walkways open to the public. There are also quiet woodlands and a fine parkland approach to Hinton Ampner on the final section of The Wayfarers Walk. In the woodland areas, some of the waymarks are obscured by new growth and a keen eye is needed to seek them out.

Picturesque watercress beds, a weir, bridge and ford over the Meon River can be viewed at the beginning or the end of the walk. The Meon is here provided with numerous diversion channels that lead water into the watercress beds hereabouts. By one or two of these channels there are also to be found 'bathing steps' where villagers could wash in the stream or draw water from the channels.

1. From Warnford Village Hall on Lippen Lane, follow the footpath sign nailed to the side of the building uphill to quickly reach the open down.

   At the top go right by the rather forbidding sign 'Please keep to the footpaths. Dogs must be kept on a lead.' Quickly pass through some young saplings and in about 100 yards go left at the yellow waymark on the telephone pole. Follow the telephone line across the field to a circular yellow waymark by the corner of the wood. Go ahead on the broad track to the next waymark on the large tree. (Ignore the 'permissive access' sign low down on the right.)

2. Go left and in 100 yards turn right through the gap in the hedge. Angle left across the field to the partly concealed circular waymark, just inside the edge of the wood ahead.

   Some 20 yards beyond this waymark encounter a signposted, double track junction. Cross this junction slightly to the right to

The picturesque bridge and ford in Warnford village

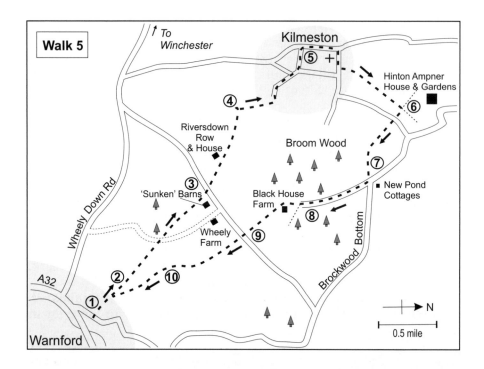

enter a large field at the waymarked power pole. Cross this very large cultivated field by lining up on the second telephone pole from the left in the centre of the field. If the field is in crops it may be difficult to discern the line of the path – but you make for the corner of the woodland by sunken barns, to the left of Wheely Farm. Exit the field in the trees and walk the few yards down to the lane.

3. **Cross the lane to the fingerpost pointing into the grounds of Riversdown House. Walk along the drive and keep right at the 'Old Stables' wall plaque, to pass the house and its beautiful formal gardens on the left.**

This ancient property is now an upmarket leisure and country club. The site is well worth a look and worthy of enquiries at the office if you fancy a few days of active country pursuits, health toning or body pampering!

Pass by tennis courts and across part of the fairway of the golf course to enter a gated opening into the woods of Riversdown Row. Pass quickly through the wood on the forest track and exit to the strongly fenced path signed cryptically by DEFRA 'This land is down to nature'. It sure is!

4. Follow the fenced path as it shoehorns you round to the right to a stile. Cross this and the following field.

   Go through a gap in the hedgerow and turn left. Keep the hedgerow on the left and follow the path as it becomes a sunken lane. It shortly reaches a lane by a cottage. Turn left on this lane that accesses Dean House on the edge of Kilmeston village. Walk up to the village passing on the left the memorial board to the fond memory of local hunting dogs.

5. At the Village Hall, turn right and walk up through Kilmeston which has some pretty cottages dotted here and there. At the red telephone box at the top of the village turn right to reach the small parish church of St Andrew.

   If the church is open you might like to look inside. The churchyard is peaceful, tree shaded, timeless.

   Just beyond the church, on the left, join the Wayfarers Walk. Follow this to cross stiles and fields as Hinton Ampner house comes into view on the hill. Cross the parkland sward to the gate at the estate boundary.

   If you wish to visit the house, gardens and tearoom proceed ahead, but you will have to return to this point to continue the walk.

6. Once through this estate gate turn right (or left if you are coming back from the house). Shortly cross a lane and continue on a level and broad gravel track, actually a 'restricted byway' which basically means that cars and trail bikes are prohibited. In just under half a mile reach a junction of metalled lanes.

7. Turn right here by the barns and head up the lane and into the woods.

48

Large brown hares live in these woods and you may be lucky enough to see one.

8. At the waymarked fork, go right on the otherwise private road to Black House farm. Cross the stile behind the farmhouse, then another one by keeping to the left edge of the field. Keep ahead to pass a strip of woodland on your right. Reach and cross the lane which is fingerposted on both sides.

9. You now have to cross one of the largest cultivated fields that it is possible for a walker to encounter.

The field is more than a half a mile wide. The route is right through the middle, and takes up to 15 minutes to cross. Wheely Farm is away on the right. The ground is soft and the field may be heavily cultivated. Do be patient and try to keep to the discernible line of path, avoiding trampling any crops that might be growing.

When you reach the trees at the far side it is worth looking back to see the ground you have traversed. Quite the daddy of a field that, was it not?

10. Pass through the trees to a sign that you will recognize as familiar. 'Please keep to the footpaths. Dogs must be kept on a lead'. Keep ahead initially around the left edge of the field. At the end of the patch of woodland continue beside the grassy bank that separates the upper and lower fields. Warnford is now back in view down to the left. Shortly reconnect with the outward route at the conspicuous telephone pole and go left back down into Warnford.

By the Way

Hinton Ampner House
Hinton Ampner House is well-up in the ranks of those iconic English stately homes surrounded by magnificent gardens. The National Trust now owns the property and it is one of Hampshire's top visitor attractions. The garden was developed by Ralph Dutton (1898-1985) the last Baron Sherborne, as a lifelong work commencing in 1930. The garden is now probably more famous than the house. Often described as a 'masterwork' of 20th century garden-design, there is an appealing wall garden and the lawns and plantings of shrubs, trees and flower-beds are

arranged in both formally classical and informal patterns. A feature for garden-minded visitors is the availability of advice from the estate gardeners.

The house was originally constructed in 1790 but remodelled in 1867. Dutton reshaped it in 1936 and 1939 to his notion of a Georgian country house. Unfortunately, it was badly damaged by fire in 1960 and had to be restored once more. The house now contains the former owner's collection of Georgian and Regency furniture, several Italian and other notable paintings, and other fine art exhibits.

www.nationaltrust.org.uk/main-hintonampnergarden Ph. 01962 771305

Watercress Beds

The still-productive watercress beds along the Meon in Warnford are an indicator of this once much larger horticultural sub-industry that flourished along the valleys of the clear and unpolluted waters of the Hampshire chalk streams, especially the Itchen and the Test.

The volunteer-maintained Mid-Hants Railway, popularly known as 'The Watercress Line' (a railway line connecting Alresford to Alton and now

The still productive watercress beds on the Meon River at Warnford

run as a tourist attraction with excursion steam trains), and the former Meon Valley Railway, were utilized for the fast transit of watercress up to Covent Garden market in London. The heyday of the industry was in late-Victorian times when watercress sandwiches were the staple at 'high teas' in popular hotels and salons of the period. The plant was also used as a vegetable as well as a salad plant. It was also eaten on the streets of the capital by early-rising workers in hand-held bunches after the manner of ice creams. An early form of fast-food giving rise to the adage 'watercress is poor man's bread'.

6: Beyond Beacon Hill –
Seeking Betty Mundy's Bottom and
a Devil's Punchbowl from Exton

Punchbowl – Nature reserve – High viewpoints

Distance	7.5 miles
Approximate time	Four hours
Start and finish	The Shoe Inn at Exton off the A32 north of Wickham. The best parking option is to use the informally named 'Millennium Trees' unsurfaced car park at the northern end of Church Lane. This is at the point where the lane joins the A32 next to the bridge carrying the main road over the Meon River. Using this car park adds about three quarters of a mile to the total walking distance. Grid reference 613208
Refreshments	The Shoe Inn at Exton
Map	OS 1:25,000 Explorer Sheet Winchester

This walk involves a steep ascent up the shoulder of Beacon Hill shortly after the start. Shorter gradients and undulations are encountered later. The walk is generally 'high-level' in character providing extensive views to central Hampshire and to the south coast. The area around Rabbit Copse is very rural and as isolated as Hampshire probably gets! The route makes use of very scenic sections of the South Downs Way and the Wayfarers Walk. The paths and tracks are usually broad and well-signed but care is needed in following the Wayfarers Walk markers in the vicinity of Betty Mundy's Bottom. An extra half-hour is needed for exploration of the Beacon

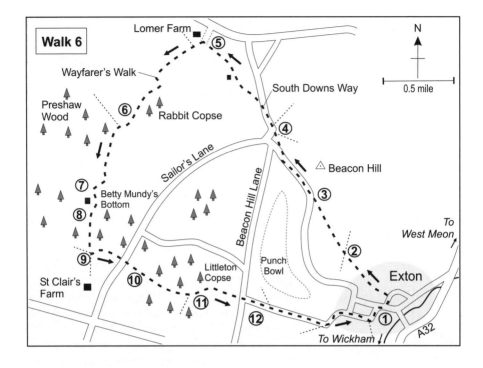

Hill National Nature Reserve. Exton is a picturesque village with some fine thatched cottages and landscaped water-gardens either side of the Meon river.

1. **With your back to The Shoe go left along Shoe Lane. Turn left at the fingerpost 'South Downs Way. Walkers'. Walk up Church Lane until it bears left. Take the footpath on the right signed 'Temporary Route for South Downs Way. Walkers Only'.**

Do not concern yourself with the word 'temporary'. The South Downs Way used to end at Burriton near Petersfield. It was later extended to Winchester and the 'temporary' word on signposts in this stretch has been around for some time whilst the authorities make small adjustments to the extension to the long-distance route.

Go through a metal gate and progress up the right side of the field. At the next fingerpost angle right across another large field still

following the signs 'South Downs Way. Walkers'. Beacon Hill looms ahead and slightly to the right.

2. Cross the waymarked stile in the hollow. Progress uphill to cross a couple of double stiles at a private road. Veer right over yet more stiles in hedges and fields to climb steeply up the left shoulder of Beacon Hill. I suggest you take this section very slowly as the gradient is steep.

Do pause to take a breath or two and admire the views back over the Meon valley. Converge with a fenced hedge on the left and as you reach the top of the hill look for the stile in the left-hand corner of the field.

3. Cross the stile into a metalled lane (The White Way). It takes about 30 minutes from the start to reach this point. Turn right up the lane. Note the great bowl of the Devil's Punchbowl to the left. In about 250 yards, as the lane levels out, there is a gap in the hedge on the right. Take this signed footpath and veer left across a field towards a gate in the far corner by the edge of the wood.

The entrance to the Beacon Hill National Nature Reserve is here. A Natural England signboard provides information about the flora and fauna and you may wish to explore the extensive beechwoods that crown the top of the hill.

4. From the car park continue ahead along the lane on the left verge still signed South Downs Way. In about 275 yards, where the lane bends right, go through the signed gate and straight ahead on the broad track.

There are views to central Hampshire from here and this is a very pleasant and peaceful section of the walk. Quintessential South Downs Way country.

Presently pass Lomer Cottage, adjacent to the site of a long-gone medieval village, and approach the cluster of buildings that make up Lomer Farm.

5. Go left between the cow sheds with the South Downs Way sign. Once across the farmyard, leave the South Downs way and go left

following the green Wayfarers Walk sign, which you will see in front of an open barn. Follow the broad farm track that is the Wayfarers Walk as it slowly descends, goes left and then right to pass Rabbit Copse.

The route follows the raised bank in the field about 60 yards from the trees. This is a very secluded, quite idyllic part of the walk. You are likely to be alone with rabbits, squirrels, occasional deer and hawks and kestrels. The hollow here is a favourite sandwich spot of mine!

6. **Cross the hollow to the stile in the conifer line ahead. Continue up the Wayfarers Walk track and bear left at the sign with Preshaw Wood now on the right. At the edge of the wood go half-right to the stile in the ribbon of woodland ahead.**

   This stile is marked by a large yellow disc on a post. Cross the stile and walk a few yards through the trees. Go right across the top of the field to the stile partly hidden in the right-hand corner. Cross it and turn left to descend into Betty Mundy's Bottom.

The walk descends into the hidden dry valley of the Devil's Punchbowl above Exton

7. **At the Bottom turn right and walk towards Betty Mundy's Cottages.**

As you will see, these are anything but cottages!

Keep left initially around the garden fence and left again into Kings Copse. Pass the wooden sign on the tree saying 'Betty Mundy's Walk'.

The Wayfarers Walk makes use of this ornamental 'three sides of a rectangle' walk around the property.

8. **At the far side of the coppice turn left with the signs through the gate. Cross the field ahead with conifer plantations 60 yards up on both the left and right sides of the field.**

9. **At the approach lane to St Clair's Farm, leave the Wayfarers Walk by turning left on to the yellow waymarked footpath. Ascend the slope keeping to the left edge of the field. At the fingerpost, cross Sailor's Lane and walk ahead to enter Littleton Copse.**

10. **Keep straight ahead through the Copse ignoring crosstracks. Rather stark red painted footpath signs here make sure you stay on the correct route! It takes about 12 minutes to reach the eastern edge of the copse, up a short slope.**

11. **Turn left at the dual yellow waymark and red footpath signs and in about 200 yards go right at the next waymark to leave the copse. At first keep to the left hand edge of the field, then go through a signed gap in the hedge to continue progress along the right hand side of the upper field.**

12. **Cross Beacon Hill Lane and take the rough lane signed 'Unsuitable for Motor Vehicles'.**

This lane takes you steeply down into the depths of the Devil's Punchbowl. The Devil is a thirsty fellow! He keeps punchbowls all over the country. Must be all that fire and brimstone down below. This one is not to be confused with the more famous one at Hindhead or the Devil's Dyke behind Brighton. The punchbowl in geographical terms is a deeply incised dry valley typical of those found throughout the chalk country. Presently reach Allens Farm Lane which leads you back into Exton.

By the Way

Beacon Hill National Nature Reserve is a botanically significant area of chalk grassland and woodland maintained by Natural England. The slopes of this prominent hill have been used for cattle and sheep pasturing for centuries. Paths which occupy hollows leading from the summit area are believed to be old drovers' routes. There is a small car park at the reserve entrance. A signboard here provides information on the natural history of the reserve. Laid out trails allow the walker to potter amongst the mature beech and hazel woods which are the habitat for small mammals and deer. Butterflies that have been sighted in the reserve include the brown argus, the Duke of Burgundy, chalk hill blues and silver spotted skippers. Relatively rare downland plants that can be found here include various types of orchids, sheep's fescue grass, rock roses, eyebrights, rampion and fleaworts.

7: High points and attractive woodlands in the Upper Meon Valley

Ups and Downs – Woodland wildlife – Forest tracks

Distance	5.5 miles
Approximate time	Two and a half hours
Start and finish	The free car park beside the village green at the end of Workhouse Lane in the village of East Meon. Grid reference 678223
Refreshments	See Walk 2
Map	OS 1:25,000 Explorer Sheet Winchester

Although not long, this is a fairly strenuous walk involving a short but steep ascent of Small Down early on in the walk. However, the paths are good and the going is generally firm. The physical effort is well worth while as the views from Small Down are stupendous and provide probably the best 360 degree prospect of the whole of the upper Meon Valley. The middle section of the walk, on a broad track, is through the fringe of the delightful Hen Wood, one of the largest areas of mixed forest in the whole of this valley.

1. Start at the 'footpath' sign in the bottom right corner of the village green adjacent to the car park. Cross the green to pass between the houses at the top.

    Cross the court behind to the right and go up Duncombe Road through newish estate houses. At the T junction opposite fields turn left for 150 yards.

2. Opposite Princes Cottage look for the dilapidated fingerpost all but lost in the hedgerow. Follow the direction indicated through the gate and across the field ahead.

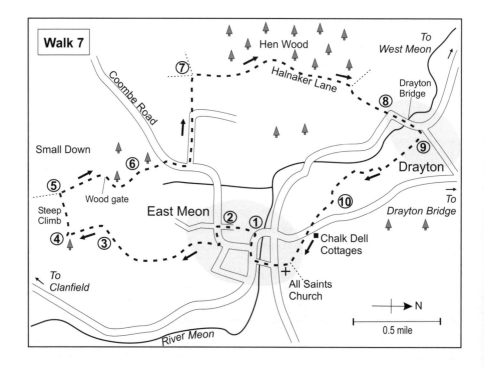

Go through the next metal gate and keep to the left side of the field. Swing right at the yellow waymark sign across the centre of this cultivated field. A series of small yellow stakes indicate the route you should follow. Go ahead at the fingerpost signed 'footpath' in the corner.

3. At the woodland cross the stile and turn up right. Go through the gate and turn left.

   At the next gate look out for a further 'lost' fingerpost inadequately located on the down slope almost in the hedge to the left. Do not go through the gate which the track tempts you to so do!

4. Facing the gate, turn right and begin the very steep climb of the flank of Small Down.

   It is quite a pull but does not take long and you should stop halfway up for a breather.

At the patch of pine trees, cross the yellow waymarked stile and proceed up onto the huge whaleback top of Small Down.

On a fine day this is the sort of place that makes you feel good to be alive. The whole of the upper Meon Valley is before, below and around you. A magic spot and if you want to linger for a picnic and drink in the views then do so with enthusiasm.

5. **Turn right (northerly) at the crest of Small Down and follow the fence line as it drops down slightly to the right to the wood, and then go right to a metal gate in the corner where the wood takes on a rough 'L' shape.**

There are 'flat' yellow waymarks here on the gatepost but you can only see them when you are right on top of them.

Enter the wood through the gate and follow the broad forest track as it winds down towards Duncoombe Cottage.

6. **At the road turn right and in about 275 yards turn left at the fingerpost onto the concrete track signed 'Forty Acres. Beerleigh Estate.'**
   Go left around the farm buildings and ahead to the prominent 'fourways' track junction.

7. **Turn right here following the sign 'Public Bridleway to East Meon. 2 miles'.**

The track (Halnaker Lane) now stretches ahead for nearly a mile through the fringes of Hen Wood. Leave the woodland track beyond the forest gate and progress along the lane to Drayton Cottages.

8. **Turn left with care along the road to cross Drayton Bridge over the Meon.**

This is one of the best places to see the meanders contained by the terraced field in the river course to the left.

9. **Keeping on the right side of the road, in about 100 yards join the signed footpath on the right that is hidden from you until you**

are on top of it. It is before the road bends left and before Drayton Farm.

Go over the stiles ahead, initially following the right side of the fields just above the river. The route then goes right down towards the river, then left along the field and then up left again to an 'exit' stile. In effect, you walk three sides of a rectangle around this field. Progress ahead up the slope and by the hedge over more stiles to reach a road.

10. Cross in front of Chalk Dell Cottages to find another stile partly hidden to the right of the drive and garden of these cottages.

Cross it and angle left across the field to the corner of the woodland garden. Cross the stile and go ahead along the garden fence to the stile beside the steps down into the churchyard of All Saints. In the churchyard descend to the first bench and turn

The Meon flows by ancient thatched buildings and under a flint bridge at Frogmore

right down to the gate in the wall. Cross the road with care and make your way along The Cross back to the car park.

By the Way

Meanders

These are bends and loops in the course of a river that are characteristic of what geographers describe as the 'mature' stage of river valley development. For such a small river, with relatively limited erosive power, the Meon shows many of the classic features of river landscape topography. Once a river has acquired sufficient volume it begins to 'sway' around the lower sections of its valley, particularly so if it encounters obstacles and banked valley sides. This fluvial action is enhanced in periods of high rainfall. At Drayton Bridge you can see evidence of this 'swaying' as the Meon bends, loops and builds meanders in a short stretch between the road on the right and the banked fields on the left. Lower down river, between Droxford and Soberton, there are even more obvious meanders and small 'ox-bow' lakes. These latter are formed when the river abandons its loops, often in times of flood as it breaks out of its banks, to straighten-up and form a new channel. The abandoned meanders become small 'ox-bows' or crescent-shaped lakes or backwaters.

7 Jan 2017 1hr 50mins

8: Striding along the South Downs Way from Meonstoke to Old Winchester Hill

Ancient hill fort – South Downs Way – Tranquil meadows

Distance	5 miles
Approximate time	Two and a half hours
Start and finish	The walk starts at The Meon Hall (the village hall) adjacent to the recreation ground at the corner of Fry's and Pound Lanes in Meonstoke. The village is off the A32 north of Droxford. Grid reference 616202
Refreshments	Village stores and Post Office in Corhampton, the immediate neighbour village to Meonstoke. The Bucks Head public house in Meonstoke
Map	OS 1:25,000 Explorer Sheet 132 Winchester

Although the distance is not great, this walk does involve a muscular, slow climb to the top of Old Winchester Hill at 648 feet above sea level. The walk is on good tracks and the ascent is well worth the effort. The walk makes good use of the South Downs Way, one of the finest long distance high-level routes (Winchester to Eastbourne) in the whole country. Meonstoke and Corhampton are twin villages separated by the Meon river here is in one of the most scenic parts of its valley. Both villages have notable historic churches.

1. From The Meon Hall turn left and walk back along Pound Lane to the bridge over the railway path. Descend to the railway path via the steps just over the bridge on the right. You have to negotiate two inconveniently located metal rails that act as a kind of default stile for the steps.Walk north along the railway path.

Shortly, keep to the left of a farm track that runs down to the right and almost immediately descend some steps on the left to the lane that goes through the 'broken' bridge.

Cross the lane and regain the railway embankment via the steps on the left.

The railway path now opens up out of the trees to provide fine views to Old Winchester Hill rising from the fields to the right.

2. **Just beyond the next bridge, leave the railway path to turn right at the fingerpost reading 'South Downs Way. Public Bridleway. Eastbourne 84 miles'.**

Don't worry – you are not going the whole way!

Immediately go down to the small footbridge over a side channel of the Meon, sometimes dry, more often a gurgling, clear stream about three yards wide, flowing over gravels than can glisten in the sunlight.

Follow the South Downs Way as it first bends sharply right from the river and then turns left to gradually climb between fields. Now follows the long, steady 'pull' to a field corner where the track goes right.

From this mid-height spot there is a fine view of Beacon Hill to the rear. The track continues as a broad, wire-fenced way generally keeping to the edge of the fields.

3. **At the point where the Monarch's Way comes in from the left there is a bit of reading to do.**

The Monarch's way fingerpost explains itself thus. 'The Monarch's Way. A 615 mile walking trail following the escape of Charles II after the Battle of Worcester in 1651'.

I know no one who has walked the full 615 miles of The Monarch's Way but it is nice to know that Charles II was an avid rambler! The route of his escape would be quite an undertaking for anyone.

Anyway, pass through the gate and note the sign that welcomes you to 'Old Winchester Hill – National Nature Reserve'. Stop briefly to read the information about the nature reserve. Now take a good

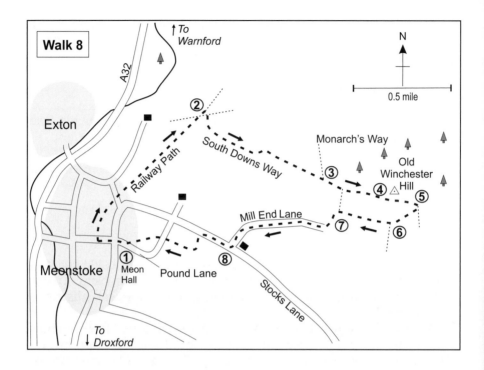

breath before you tackle the final, steep section to the top through the patch of mixed woodland.

4. **Go through a gate onto the open hillside and proceed up to the trig column set in the centre of the ramparts of the ancient hill fort.**

The earthworks of the hill fort dominate the summit of Old Winchester Hill. You can explore the ramparts at leisure. Many people who make the effort to come up here like to complete the full circuit of the outer ramparts.

Next to the trig column is a stone plinth with a metal view finder plate on top. Without question, the views from here are some of the finest in Hampshire. On a clear day the chimney of Fawley Power Station, near Calshot, is visible 16 miles away. Another Beacon Hill (not to be confused with the one just across the valley) near Highclere, can be seen some 25 miles to the north almost on the

Hampshire-Berkshire border. Chichester Harbour to the east, and the Isle of Wight to the south across The Solent are also in view.

Look in a north, north-easterly direction and see if you can spot the spire of Privett Church just above the trees at four and a half miles distance.

5. **From the trig column cross the hill fort on the main path in a generally easterly direction.**

Note the deep partially wooded coombe dropping to the left, so typical a feature of the chalk country.

Leave the reserve by the eastern gate – there is a memorial bench here and a diorama plinth that models the dwellings and layout of the hill fort as it might have appeared thousands of years ago.

6. **Turn immediately right at the fingerpost reading 'South Downs Way'. Pass alongside a newly planted vineyard and, keeping it on your left, drop steeply down to the gate in the hedge.**
   Turn right with the South Downs Way fingerpost to walk along the right hand edge of a large field above Stocks Cottage. Go straight ahead at the next fingerpost still on the South Downs Way. Now the track is a five yards wide 'greenway' between a hedge on the left and a fence on the right.

7. **At the end of the greenway, leave the South Downs Way by turning left at the 'Public Bridleway' fingerpost.**
   Descend the short distance to a prominent line of conifers. Turn right still following the bridleway. This remains a track but it assumes the title of Mill End Lane. Follow it to the junction of Stocks Lane.

8. **Turn right here along the metalled lane, which is high edged and has no verges. It is a quiet lane but you do need to keep a lookout for traffic. At a house on the right, after about 300 yards, turn left at the footpath sign.**
   Go a quarter right/diagonally across the field to the stile in the corner. Cross it and follow the left-hand edge of the field over another stile. Reach a lane and cross it.
   Go over the stile and, though the waymark points directly

The trig point and diorama plinth amongst burial mounds on the top of Old Winchester Hill

ahead across the field, the well-established and bootmarked route goes slightly to the left actually keeping to the fence line at the left-hand edge of this arable field. You encounter houses with long gardens over the fences to the left. At the end of these cross yet another stile and veer left across the final field to the stile in the corner at the junction of Fry's Lane and Pound Lane.

By the Way

The summit of Old Winchester Hill is crowned by an ancient and impressively bulky hill fort, the main structures of which are believed to date from the Iron Age. The earthen ramparts of the hill fort cover some 14 acres and, like those of Maiden Castle in Dorset and Cissbury Ring in West Sussex, circle the summit offering remarkable evidence of early forms of defensive settlement and civil engineering! The high open site, with views to the coast would have provided a good lookout for the approach of unwelcome guests and interlopers bent on serious land-grabbing. The site has not been fully excavated archeologically, though sporadic diggings and explorations have taken place down the years and there is some evidence for Celtic occupation at one time. The site reveals historical stages or 'overlappings' in its construction and use. The ramparts enclose much older Bronze Age barrows or burial mounds from the period 4500-3500 BC. Sometimes referred to as the 'hill cemetery', these barrows are a central feature on top of the hill and are often used, possibly irreverently, as sunbathing places by visitors on warm, sunny days. There are two entrances or 'gates' to the hill-fort on an east-west axis. Adjacent to the eastern entrance is a signboard with archeological information as-known; and a somewhat speculative graphical, diorama of how the former settlers on the hill might have constructed dwellings within the ramparts. During World War II the hill was a mortar testing range and it is possible that there are still items of unexploded ordnance about. It is therefore advisable not to wander about in the fenced-off areas around the hill.

9: Drifting along low ways and high ways near Brockbridge

Water mill – Saxon church – Roman relics

Distance	8 miles
Approximate time	Three and a half hours
Start and finish	Bus stop and shelter in front of The Manor House on South Hill (A32) in the centre of Droxford. Adjacent parking in front of the church. An additional car park is on Union Lane next to the fire station. Grid reference 605182
Refreshments	See Walks 8 and 10
Map	OS 1:25,000 Explorer Sheet 119 Meon Valley

This is a walk that shortly after its start crosses the attractive mill-race on the Meon river in Droxford. The route then leads up a lane to Brockbridge and on established paths through woods on the right bank of the river to Meonstoke and Corhampton. A visit to the Saxon church at Corhampton involves a short diversion. Later, the walk winds up to the high and airy downs and secluded woodlands to the east of Brockbridge. Short stretches of quiet country lanes are used to connect footpaths and bridleways. Towards the end of the walk there is an unavoidable half-mile stretch on the aptly named Long Road. This is however, an attractive country road with walkable grass verges. Do anticipate meeting two or three vehicles on this stretch and take care accordingly. The walk draws to a close by using the line of The Driftway, an ancient chalky track between fields and farms, over Little Common Down.

1. Walk north from the bus stop and in a few yards turn right into Mill Lane.

Take the Wayfarers Walk signed path to the right of the mill, cross the mill race, and continue alongside the river.

You may well be able to see trout in the sparkling waters here.

Cross the footbridge and continue on the extension of Mill Lane up to Brockbridge Road.

2. **Cross the road to the fingerpost signed 'footpath' and climb the steps made up from timber railway sleepers.**
   Continue ahead through the wood with glimpses of the river down the bank to your left. When you come up to join Brockbridge Road, go left for about 200 yards to the metal fingerpost on the left signed 'public footpath'. Follow this fenced path to Meonstoke School.

Walk up through the village passing the impressive thatched barn, now used for community events. The village architecture of Meonstoke is generally pleasing to the eye and it includes mellow brick houses, thatched cottages and larger Georgian-style mansions.

3. **At the cross-roads go left with the 'Corhampton ¼' sign to pass The Bucks Head pub. Cross the river and go right at the A32 to visit Corhampton Church. After your visit, return to the cross-roads in Meonstoke.**
   Go in the direction of the sign 'Pound Lane ½'. Walk up Pound Lane to pass The Meon Hall on the right. Where Pound Lane turns sharply left, go right onto the track and almost immediately left at the fingerpost signed 'Restricted Bridleway'. This ascends gradually then swings right and climbs more steeply to the vicinity of Pondside Farm at the top of the hill.

4. **Turn left along the lane. Just past the mobile phone tower, turn left at the yellow waymarked post signed 'footpath'.**
   Cross the stiles at the lane and continue diagonally across the field to the barn. Go round it on the left. Cross the lane at the fingerpost by a cottage and go ahead along the formal drive to Stokewood.
   At the entrance gate to this 'big house' – a classically elegant

property – take the white gate in the hedge on the right to follow the fenced path that leads you around the gardens of the house.

Beyond the property, continue ahead on the track that borders woodland and swings right in a more southerly direction.

5. At the waymarked post by the field gate do not turn left. It is easy to make a navigational mistake here. Especially as the idyllic farm country hereabouts tends to capture your attention. The correct route is straight ahead.

As you enter the wood go right and immediately left with the waymarks.

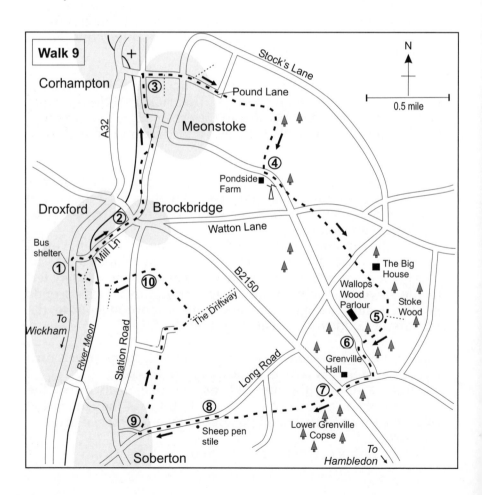

The 1000 year old Saxon church at Corhampton

You may have to step over a wire with a laconic message on it. 'Non electric – but please don't tell the cows'. Yes – quite!

Progress through this quiet and shady stretch of Stoke Wood. Yellow topped posts mark the route through the trees. You may well choose to eat a packed lunch in these shady groves. There are lots of felled logs to sit upon.

6. **Exit to the road below Wallops Wood Parlour.**

Yes – it is called that but please don't ask!

Go left along the lane. Turn right at the junction and pass the attractive flint walls of Grenville House and stables to reach the B2150.

7. **Cross this busy 'B' road slightly to the left to the fingerpost signed 'footpath'. Cross the stile here and go ahead along the edge of Lower Grenville Copse.**

At the waymarks at the edge of the copse, veer right to cross the field (it may be ploughed or cultivated) to the stile visible on the far side.

Cross both the stiles at the bridleway here and continue down the wide grassy field. There may well be flocks of sheep in it.

8. Exit to Long Road by a well-constructed, two-stepped stile by a small sheep enclosure. Turn left and go down Long Road for half a mile.

It is a pleasant road to walk along but it does carry a bit more traffic than most of the country lanes around this area.

It has walkable grass verges which you should follow to a point about 150 yards just beyond the village entry sign reading 'Soberton'. There are two fingerposts on the right both signed 'footpath'.

9. Go acutely right over the stile. Progress up the field alongside the tree-line on the left. Cross another stile and progress to the end of the field. Cross the stile here and enter The Driftway. It takes you ahead then right and left. Almost at the centre of Little Common Down turn left. There is no post or waymark at this point. However, the route is clear being a three yards wide grassy sward between cultivated fields. When you reach the trees, go left and down to the stile into the road.

10. Turn left for 20 yards along the road. Then turn right at the sign 'Bridleway'. Pass over the old railway bridge and go left through the swing gate. Go ahead to the tree corner and pass through two more swing gates. Go down to cross the Meon river on the footbridge and re-enter Droxford by the churchyard path.

By the Way

Corhampton Church is a Saxon church dating from about 1020 and built in the reign of Canute. To stand in front of this ancient, unadorned but somehow powerfully symbolic building, and to realize that people worshipped here prior to the Tudors, the Crusades and the Norman Conquest is thought provoking indeed. I challenge you to remain unmoved! The building is unique in not being dedicated to a

Christian saint. It is simply 'Corhampton Church' and was ever thus. The church is usually open in daylight hours and you should take the opportunity to visit the simple nave. Here you will find original frescoes on the walls near the altar showing the expulsion from the Garden of Eden on one side, and the traditional story of St Swithun working a miracle to restore eggs broken as a basket fell from the hands of a peasant woman. The churchyard is dominated by a magnificent yew tree, that great signifier of English churchyards. Also on the mound here is a Roman sarcophagus, one of many Roman relics found in this part of the Meon valley.

Roman sarcophagus used for 'horticultural purposes' on Corhampton church mound

10: Finding traces of D Day on the railway path at Droxford

D Day – Meon Valley Railway – Surprise views

Distance	6.6 miles
Approximate time	Three hours
Start and finish	Churchyard precinct of St Mary and All Saints in Droxford, on the A32 north of Wickham. Grid reference 606182
Refreshments	The White Horse and The Bakers Arms in Droxford. Post Office convenience store attached. The Hurdles pub close to the end of the walk
Map	OS 1:25,000 Explorer Sheet 119 Meon Valley

A walk on very good paths and bridle ways and making use of a long section of railway path. There is only one modest gradient leading to scenic landscape viewpoint. There are several short sections using metalled country lanes which have no pavements or roadside paths. Whilst these are generally quiet, vehicles should always be anticipated and care should be taken. The busy A32 has to be crossed twice.

1. With your back to The Wayfarers Walk double fingerpost in the churchyard precinct, walk past the church tower on your left, to go through the iron picket gate in front of you. Take the path ahead.

   In 200 yards or so cross the stile into a field and proceed ahead keeping the fence on the left. Cross another stile by some houses. Now walk along the right-hand edge of the field for two thirds of its length. As it broadens out into a paddock, often with horses contentedly grazing, continue straight ahead on the path as it moves to the left-hand side of the field. Leave this field through the metal gate in the left-hand corner, just above a bend in the Meon River, at a location known as Cut Bridge.

2. **Turn right up the lane for about 200 yards to reach the A32.**

This lane only takes a minute or two to negotiate but it is high hedged and banked and offers no footpath so please do take care.

Cross the A32 and continue up the lane past Midlington Barns.

Just on the right here is an alpaca farm. You may be able to see these unusual but attractive animals grazing in the fields.

The lane now veers to the left.

3. **Shortly, at the Midlington Farm gate, turn left onto the track (a 'Green Lane' and higher up a permissive bridleway).**

This initially hugs the foot of the slope above fields. Then it gradually contours upwards through a wooded area. Now for a very pleasant surprise! You emerge from the trees onto the open side of the hill by a bench. Stop and sit here for a while. There are wonderful views over the Meon Valley, to Soberton opposite, and south towards the Isle of Wight.

Continue ahead to pass a signpost on your right reading 'Allan Kings Way'. Go through a belt of trees and across a broad field with power lines straight ahead. Gradually descend to Cott Street.

This is an unlikely name for an airy and open, metalled country lane.

4. **Turn left here down to the A32 again.**

Cross the the main road and descend to cross the Meon over the permanently signed 'Weak Bridge'. Walk up to the old railway bridge ahead. Climb the steps on the left-hand side to reach the

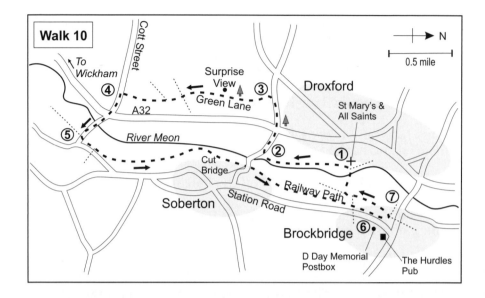

embankment top. This was the central section of the Meon Valley Railway (MVR) line.

5. **You now turn left and follow the railway path in a northerly direction for just over two miles.**

There are benches along the way, and some good views over tranquil stretches of the meandering Meon down to your left. The river even provides an example of what geographers call an 'Ox Bow Lake' (a mini meander abandoned by the river as it attempts to straighten its course). There are good picnic spots along here and you may be lucky enough to spot a heron or a kingfisher swooping above the river. The route is beautifully wooded and alternately passes through old cuttings and over embankments.

When an old bridge appears continue under it.

After about 12 minutes walking from this bridge, you will pass under another such bridge. Shortly, you will come to a wooden fence (on your right) enclosing the quite well-preserved platforms of the old Droxford railway station. Directly opposite the old station building, now a private house with much railway restoration memorabilia adorning it, is a waymark on the left.

6. **Turn down right on the short track to the road. Go carefully to the right under the bridge and turn right by The Hurdles pub.**

A few yards up on the right, just before the old railway station building is a familiar red pillar box. Somewhat bizarrely, set into its base is the wooden plaque explaining how Winston Churchill and Dwight D. Eisenhower and other World War II leaders spent days in a railway carriage here backed into a siding, whilst they deliberated plans for D Day and the eventual liberation of Europe.

7. **Retrace your steps under the bridge to Brockbridge Cottage at the top of Mill Lane. Which is signed as 'No Through Road.'**

A few yards down on the left, partly hidden in the bushes, are two waymarks, the yellow Hampshire county one, and a green one reading 'Wayfarers Walk – Circular Route'. Take this path as it passes behind cottages. Ignore the first waymarked path on the right. Continue ahead on this hedgerow path with Meon meadows down to the right. In about 10 minutes you reach a stile-gate and you turn right here to cross two channels of the

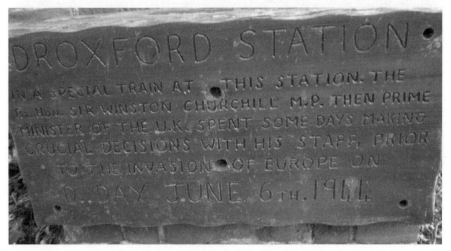

The D Day sign on the pillar box in front of old Droxford station on the MVR

Meon on wooden footbridges. Your starting point of the churchyard of St Mary and All Saints is just ahead.

By the Way

The Meon Valley Railway (MVR) ran from Alton to Fareham with onward connections to Gosport and Stokes Bay for steamers to the Isle of Wight. In essence the line was an alternative London-South Coast route competing with the Portsmouth to London Waterloo and Southampton to London main lines via Winchester and Basingstoke. Initially conceived as a dual track route, it was eventually built by the London and South Western Railway Company (LSWR) with only one track. Bridges and tunnels though, were built to accommodate dual track running. Unquestionably one of the most picturesque railway routes in the south of England, it opened to passengers on 1st June in 1903. Sadly, it never fulfilled commercial promises and never carried sufficient passengers to bring it into year-on profits. There were intermediate stations and halts at Farringdon, Tisted, Privett,

Nature has reclaimed West Meon station on the old Meon Valley Railway line

West Meon, Droxford, Mislingford and Wickham. The line enjoyed brief periods of prosperity and a kind of fame. Prior to 1920, goods trains carried produce from the extensive market gardens in the southern districts. Whole trains of strawberries were loaded at Mislingford and Wickham. Milk trains and cattle trucks were also early 'specials'. During both world wars the line was used by troop trains bound for the ports. After 1920, ever increasing competition from the roads reduced the status of the line to that of a rural branch line. It closed to passengers on 5 February 1955. Goods services lingered on until 1968. A short life of just over 50 years for 22.5 miles of line!

11: Byways and bridle ways on the route from Soberton to Lower Grenville Copse

Country pub – Naval history – Pheasant woods

Distance	5.4 miles
Approximate time	Two and a half hours
Start and finish	The White Lion public house in Soberton. Reached via a side road off the A32 just before Droxford. There is a layby for parking at the cross-roads near the village hall. Grid reference 611166
Refreshments	The White Lion has a restaurant and a beer garden. Nearest shops are in Droxford
Map	OS 1:25,000 Explorer Sheet 119 Meon Valley

The route makes use of established and well-signed footpaths and bridleways. There are no significant difficulties underfoot but there are two modest gradients, firstly up Soberton Down and later up East Hoe Road. However, the sunken bridleway section north of Shere Copse is susceptible to falls of trees growing precariously up on the earth banks. Any track blockages caused by these should not though, seriously impede your progress. There is a short main road section alongside the B2150 where you can walk on the verge on the right. This is followed by a longer, but very pleasant ascent of East Hoe Road (in reality a quiet country lane), which also has good grass verges to walk on. Before starting the walk proper, it is worthwhile to visit the village church of St Peter's just behind the pub. In the churchyard is a very interesting example of a Roman stone coffin found in field near Broom farm in 1880. Archeological evidence of Roman buildings has been found in the vicinity of the mid-point on this walk.

1. From the Wayfarers Walk signpost (signed 'Emsworth 17 M'), which is on the road corner adjacent to The White Lion, walk down School Hill to the cross-roads.

    Carefully cross here and proceed up the lane opposite signed 'Hoe Cross 2'. In approximately 250 yards, as the lane climbs, turn left at The Wayfarers Walk sign.

    Do not be nonplussed by the track appearing to enter the drive of a property. The track crosses the drive and goes through the stile on the right which is initially hidden from view. You now climb up on to Soberton Down.

There are very fine views here. The village and church tower, often bedecked with the flag of St George nestle neatly below. Beyond Soberton, across the Meon river, is Droxford and in the middle distance, the prominent bulk of Beacon Hill.

2. Beyond the crest of the Down, pass through the gap in the hedge next to the stile.

    Continue ahead with a hedge on your left. At the end of the hedge, turn right following The Wayfarers Walk sign. There is now a ribbon of woodland on your left. In a further 250 yards turn left at the next signpost. Continue ahead on the now wooded path. Shortly, a farm track enters from the right. From here it is about 100 yards to a point where the path bends right to a memorial gate. Note this as you will come through it on the return leg.

Just before the memorial gate is a signpost with four waymarks on it, green arrows for The Waywarers Walk and Soberton Millennium Trail, yellow for the Allan King's Way, and blue for a bridleway maintained by the Countryside Service of Hampshire County Council. It is worth studying the conventions and colours of these waymarks for a moment or two.

3. **You now walk north on the blue signed bridleway with Shere Copse on your right.**

Around Shere Copse you can expect to see pheasants.Listen for the sound of woodpeckers, cuckoos and many other birds of the woodland also.

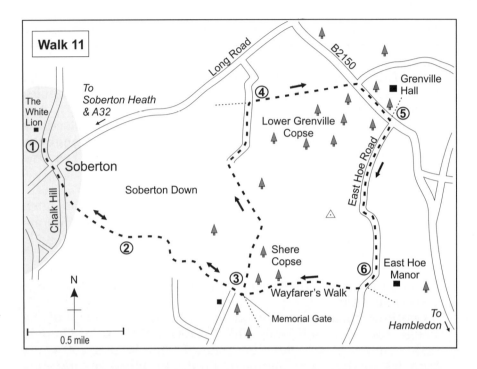

Beyond the two metal farm gates on your right, the bridleway starts to descend the eastern end of Soberton Down and becomes a 'sunken' track.

In mid-January the author had to negotiate three fallen trees here after heavy snows of the previous week. This is though a short section, and you soon reach the foot of the scarp where you are confronted by open fields and wide vistas with attractive farm houses dotted here and there.

The bridleway swings to the right and you follow it until you reach yellow waymarked stiles in both the left and right hand fences.

4. **Climb the stile to the right and cross the field to Lower Grenville Copse.**
   The path keeps to the left edge of the copse to the B2150. Cross the stile and walk on the right hand verge of this busy main road for about 300 yards.

5. **Just beyond the crest, turn right into East Hoe Road.**

This country lane is usually quiet but do anticipate meeting the occasional private car, delivery van or farm tractor. That said, this is a delightful lane. It really is! It climbs steadily to the skyline giving you wonderful views down to the Hambledon Valley on the left. Watch out for rabbits in the intriguing hollows in the side of Home Down, above Three Corners on your left. The road bends left and right and, in the vicinity of East Hoe Manor, there are long views to the south coast and the Isle of Wight in the far distance.

6. **Just at the bend in the road, a short distance from the Manor, you will re-encounter The Wayfarers Walk. Turn right to cross the field to the eastern edge of Shere Copse.**
   Continue to follow The Wayfarers Walk along the southern edge of the Copse and very soon reach the previously mentioned memorial gate at the junction of four routes. You rejoin the outward route here. Soberton is about twenty minutes walking from this point.

Four waymarks on the way to Lower Grenville Copse

By the Way
For such a tiny village, Soberton has remarkable connections with the Royal Navy.

One of the RN's and Britain's most famous sailors, Admiral of the Fleet George Anson (1697-1762) took the title 1st Baron of Soberton, even though the family seat was Shugborough in Staffordshire. Anson became famous for his circumnavigation of the globe and his leadership of the Royal Navy during the Seven Years

War. Amongst other achievements he participated in the rank of commodore in attacks on Spanish possessions in South America in the War of Jenkins Ear. As First Lord of the Admiralty, Anson oversaw the transfer of the Royal Marines to the navy from the army, promoted new uniforms for officers, and was instrumental in the expansion of ship numbers and manpower to counteract French threats in the English Channel and the Western Approaches.

The large castle-like building best viewed from the field behind the church in Soberton, is Soberton Towers built in the late 19th century. The dominant building of the village, it has been a private residence, a school, and in 1943 it became a resident hostel for members of the Womens Royal Naval Service (WRENS) serving at HMS Mercury.

HMS Soberton, one of a class of Royal Navy ships named after villages with names ending in 'ton', was a TON class minesweeper of 360 gross tonnage. She joined the Fleet List in 1957 and served her entire career in the Fishery Protection Squadron. She decommissioned in 1991 and was sold to be eventually scrapped in Belgium in 1993.

The surprise view: Soberton Down on a fine day in winter

12: The Wayfarers Walk and Green Lanes to an archer's pub at Dundridge

Wayfarers Walk – Archers heroine – Conservation Walks

Distance	8 miles
Approximate time	Four hours
Start and finish	The bus stop in Droxford across the road from the church on the corner of South Hill (A32) and Park Lane. The village centre car park is across the road here. There is another car park next to the fire station in Union Lane. Grid reference 605182
Refreshments	Droxford pubs. The Hampshire Bowman is located just over half-way in the secluded hamlet of Dundridge
Map	OS 1:25,000 Explorer Sheet 119 Meon Valley

This is a longer walk that crosses open downland farmed in traditional ways. There are fields and paddocks occupied by sheep, cows (and bulls!), and different breeds of ponies and even alpacas. This is good grazing country. The area also includes secluded woodland, managed coppices and impressively sized estate farms. There are lots of ups and downs but no real difficulties. There are however, numerous stiles to negotiate and not all of them are in good condition. At the halfway mark there is a short stretch of the busy B3035 to walk beside. Lunch can be taken in or adjacent to the archer's pub The Hampshire Bowman at Dundridge.

1. **Walk up Park lane. Cross Union Lane and continue ahead.**

   Note The Wayfarers Walk marker on the telephone pole on the right corner. Keep a lookout for such markers as you go.

Pass Droxford Junior School and at the open field continue straight ahead following The Wayfarers Walk. Ascend the slope towards Fir Down.

2. **At the wood that covers the steep side of Fir Down, go through the gate and turn right with The Wayfarers Walk sign.**

Pass through the trees and the path opens up along the flank of Fir Down. This hillside retains a largely 'unimproved' state. That is, traditional pasture on which sheep graze freely and upon which native chalk grassland plants can flourish.

Go through a gate and stay on the path round the right edge of the field.
Reach a wood (just before the road) and leave The Wayfarers Walk by turning left at the yellow waymarked post just in the corner of the wood. Go up through the trees to enter a field above a moto-cross circuit. Keep to the left side of this field until half-way across. Then go right at the fence in the centre of the field and left to reach a lane.

3. **Cross the lane to the 'bridleway' sign and continue between fields.**

The fields are actually a large horse training paddock on the left, and a pasture on the right which may well have bulls in it. A sign says so! The path is well hedge-fenced and you should not experience any difficulty from aggressive animals.

4. **Swing left into the trees at the end of the horse paddock.**

You now pass along the top of Shepherds Down and you can see where your route ahead lies in the valley below. This is a most picturesque spot.

At the end of the Shepherds Down ridge section you come to an unsigned track junction.

A typical memorial gate on the well-signposted Wayfarers Walk

This is just below stable buildings in the paddock up to your left.
5. These help you to confirm your location. The paths are clearly marked on the OS Explorer Sheet 119.

Turn right here and descend Shepherds Down to a lane. Follow this lane around the bend to reach the yellow waymark by the 'Hazel Holt Farm' sign. Turn right along the farm access track. Pass the impressive mansion of Hazel Holt on the left to enter managed woodland. Go ahead through the wood to pass a cottage on the left just before you reach the B3035.

6. **Turn left here along the road (walk on the left-hand grass verge as the road is quite busy for a 'B' road) for five minutes. You will come upon (quite suddenly) a fingerpost on the left pointing back into the wood.**
   Go left with this fingerpost into the wood and quickly exit it at a stile.

If you have brought a picnic or sandwich lunch with you this makes quite a good lunch place.

You are faced now with a very large field. Cross to the far left corner, following the left-hand edge of the field. Cross the waymarked stile.

This stile was in poor condition when I last crossed it. It was in need of some basic, remedial carpentry.

Keep ahead through a rather primeval-looking coppice to a field. Go left with the 'bridleway' sign. The long arc of woodland covering Galley Down is up to your right.

7. **At the end of the bridleway join Dundridge Lane and walk down to the hamlet of Dundridge.**

Here you will find The Hampshire Bowman and welcome refreshment. The pub has a pleasant beer garden and childrens play area adjacent to the butts and the archers' clubhouse to the side. If the club is holding a shoot, or if members are at practice on the butts, you can spend a pleasing half hour or so watching the ancestors of the yeomen of England demonstrate their skills at this most ancient of martial arts.

8. **At the cross roads just beyond the pub go in the direction of the road signpost 'Up Swanmore' for about 50 yards. Turn left at the finger post onto a concrete track that leads into a stable yard that you cross. Climb the stile by the house. And the next one! And the next one into the wood.**

These yards and paddocks will almost certainly have foals, horses and show ponies (Highland or Shetland or similar breed) in them. Try to avoid spooking the animals by walking slowly and deliberately to each stile.

9. **Once over the stile into the wood, turn right. Keep left at the 'Damson Hill' sign and progress up through this pleasant mixed woodland. Pass a red metal post and exit to a lane.**

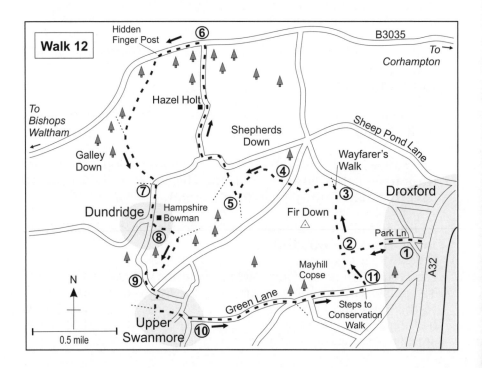

Go left along the lane to the road sign 'Dundridge ½. Swanmore 1. Park Lane'. Cross the waymarked stile on the right just past the junction. Pass down the field.

You can see Bishops Waltham ahead and low down. The chimney of Fawley Power Station is conspicuous in the distance.

Half-way down the field cross the stile in the hedgerow on the left. Go over yet another stile to a large field. This is crossed to a stepped stile at a 'triangular' road junction just in front of a prominent, double-gated house (Pond Cottage).

10. Walk on the lane between Pond Cottage on your left and the red letter box on your right. In front of Dahlia Cottage swing right and ahead onto a 'Green Lane'.

You follow this as it winds and undulates for half a mile or so. You will enjoy the long views down to the Solent on the right.

11. The Green Lane ends at a minor road and you turn left here to ascend a little to pass Mayhill Copse. Keep straight ahead at the junction (Cathedral Farm) and 'crest' the eastern edge of Fir Down. Start to descend.

Droxford now comes delightfully back into view tucked way down into the landscape below. You may like to look for alpacas in the fields to your right here.

Half-way down the lane, turn left at the fingerpost and descend the steep flight of steps to the field.

Continue straight ahead to rejoin the outward route (Wayfarers Walk) by the trees, where you turn right down to Droxford.

By the Way

In recent years the arable fields below Fir Down were included in the Conservation Walks programme. The Conservation Walks initiative of DEFRA in conjunction with local farmers, landowners and local councils represents an attempt to 'harmonize' and 'reconcile' the outdoor interests of the general public with the interests of the rural community, especially farmers. The idea is that paths are provided for people to walk freely around the edges of productive fields. Such paths supplement gazetted public rights of way. Making farmland available for access in this way is designed to encourage people to engage in crop recognition, to improve their understanding of food production techniques, educate them into the ways of the countryside. To wit – to bring all parties together in the spirit of sustainable rural development and conservation.

The Hampshire Bowman

This traditional country pub is located in the tiny hamlet of Dundridge, well off the beaten track, but very popular nonetheless. The current building, built of locally produced red bricks and Victorian in appearance, is about 130 years old. It was rebuilt after fire claimed an earlier construction and records suggest that this was the site of a rural hostelry and coaching inn for several hundred years. Quite where the

The Hampshire Bowman at Dundridge

'coaches' would have been going to from this isolated spot is a matter of curious conjecture! However, the nearby cart track up the steepish Damson Hill would probably have required horse watering and stabling hereabouts to serve local farms and the villagers.

In modern times the pub is home to active community events, hosts the Portuguese Racing Sardine Club (!!), and claims its fair share of 'mad' customers. The pub has an unusually appealing website (address below) and claims to serve 'real ale to real people'!

A heroine!

The pub has not always been called The Hampshire Bowman. Former names included The Cat and Fiddle and The Jubilee Tavern for Queen Victoria's jubilee. The pub's direct connection with the sport of archery is fairly recent. Carol Montagu, wife of the licensee in the 1970s, was a Hampshire county champion and Olympic standard archer. She helped to found and became secretary to the Merdon Bowmen, the adjacent archery club. Carol was born with a congenital heart defect and struggled to lead a normal life. She refused to allow it to interfere with her archery passions, being prominent in the Southern Counties Archery Society and taking part in county and national competitions. She died at the young age of 32 shortly after giving birth to a much-desired son, Edward. Her husband, Stan Montagu, renamed the pub in his wife's honour and created the commemorative Pinemont (Carol's maiden and married names) archery trophy to be contested annually.

www.hampshirebowman.com

13: A criss-cross woodland stroll around Upperford Copse in the Forest of Bere

Forest Commission – Royal hunting grounds – Grotto stream

Distance	2.7 miles
Approximate time	One and a half hours
Start and finish	The Forestry Commission Car Park and picnic grounds at Upperford Copse in the Forest of Bere, on Heath Road off the A32 just beyond The Roebuck Inn north of Wickham. Grid reference 589134
Refreshments	The Roebuck Inn, a short distance from the start of the walk on the A32,is a well-known and patronized gastro pub
Map	OS 1: 25,000 Explorer Sheet 119 Meon Valley

This is a nice and easy woodland stroll on well-made footpaths through part of what is known as the 'West Walk' section of the ancient Forest of Bere. Sections of the tracks are accessible to wheelchair users. Wooden benches, some of them donated as family memorials, can be found at various vantage point in the woods. It is good to stop at these for a while and to spot woodland flowering plants such as the wood anemones, bluebells and wild daffodils that can grow in profusion here. The walk is 'criss-cross' in that a loose figure-of-eight pattern is followed through the Upperford Copse and across Heath Road into the Woodend picnic area. This is a good starter walk for small children. The grotto-like stream area below Woodend is a particularly popular spot with children in the spring and summer. The walk is especially recommended for those seasons when the trees are in new leaf and the woodland flowers are in first bloom. However winter walks here can

*be very rewarding also. If you do go in late January/February say, look
out for the clusters of snowdrops on sheltered earth banks.*

1. **In the car park go over to the signboard headed 'Welcome to
West Walk' and take note of the general pattern of tracks in the
woods here – they all start and finish at the car park – but the
first part of this walk is a big circle around the woods of
Upperford Copse. From the signboard take the path immediately
on the right.**
   You will shortly come to a bench on the right at cross-tracks.

   You will pass this bench three times on this walk. It may even
   become a 'friend' if your sense of direction is a problem!

2. **Go straight ahead at these cross-tracks. Shortly, at the fork, go
left with the path as it starts to go downhill. The path bends left**

This Forestry Commission sign in Upperford Copse helps you check your location in
the ancient Forest of Bere

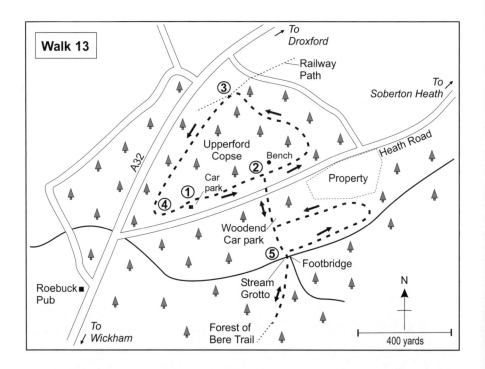

Walk 13

To Droxford

Railway Path

To Soberton Heath

Heath Road

Upperford Copse

Bench

Car park

Property

① ② ③ ④ ⑤

Woodend Car park

Footbridge

Stream Grotto

Roebuck Pub

To Wickham

Forest of Bere Trail

N

400 yards

and reaches a cross-track. Turn right and soon come to an old brick railway bridge.

3. Turn left here at the 'Forestry Commission Upperford Copse' sign and walk along the railway path for a few hundred yards.

At the next old railway bridge go left through the wooden post-rails and some 20 yards beyond the 'Forestry Commission' sign turn right at the T junction. Walk ahead and swing left with the path at a group of very tall conifers back to Upperford Copse car park.

4. Cross the car park once more and continue on the outward route as far as the bench. This time turn right and go through the wooden gate. Cross Heath Road with care to the waymarked path that leads into Woodend Car Park.

Cross to the 'Welcome to West Walk' sign and again read the information provided about West Walk by the Forestry

Commission. Go ahead to the sign 'Forest of Bere Trail. You are leaving Woodend' and follow the path a short way downhill to the wooden bridge over the stream.

Take some quality time out here to explore this delightful nook. If you have children with you, get them to count how many different mini-beasts they can find living in and beside the water. You might be surprised by what they come up with. As a cue put this poser to them: Do dragons fly?

5. Retrace your steps from the wooden bridge for just a few yards and turn right on the path that leads almost immediately over a stone culvert. Follow the path gently uphill.

    At the first cross-track turn left. Keep straight ahead at the fork to reach a broad, gravel road. Turn left over another stream and in 150 yards, by the gate leading into a small field behind a house, turn left into the wood again. Keeping the property fence on your right, go right and then left back into Woodend Car Park. Retrace your outward route to re-cross Heath Road and to turn left at the now-familiar bench back into Upperford Copse Car Park.

By The Way

The West Walk, north of Fareham, is the largest remaining part of the ancient Forest of Bere. Some 350 hectares of this once 'Royal' forest, formerly used for hunting deer and wild boar and for providing sturdy timbers for the Royal Navy in the time of 'wooden walled' frigates and ships-of-the-line, is actively managed by the Forestry Commission for England. The forest would once have been much more extensive occupying a large area inland from around Kings Somborne in the west to Rowlands Castle in south-central Hampshire. The Saxon nobility used the forest prior to its declaration as a 'Royal Reserve' under the Normans. Like the much larger New Forest (now one of England's newest national parks) to the west of Southampton, the Forest of Bere had its own laws and a Court of Verderers and was legally separated from Common Law. It is not clear to what extent monarchs and members of the aristocracy used the forest in the medieval period. King Charles I is reputed to have been the last monarch to have actively hunted in the forest in 1628. In the 17th century the area of woodland began to diminish largely owing to the demand for timber from shipbuilders on the nearby coast and river inlets, and from settlement and agricultural encroachment. However, Samuel Pepys still preferred to avoid its depths when travelling towards Havant in 1662. Presumably because he feared the forest concealed wild beasts and even wilder backwoodsmen!

The forest contains examples of many British broadleaved woodland trees, including old oaks that escaped the attentions of the axemen in former centuries. As part of its productive forestry remit, the Forestry Commission also maintains copses of rapidly growing young conifers here. However, these are apparently being phased out in favour of new, broadleaved plantings. The West Walk is an important 'outdoor lung' for people living quite close-by in the urban areas of Portsmouth, Southampton, Locks Heath and Fareham in particular. It is well-managed for visitors and the Forestry Commission has its own system of trail markers. Signboards in the car park and picnic areas provide details of plants, flowers and animal life.

14: Wickham walkabout and memories of a famous naval battle

Meon Valley Trail – West Walk picnic area – Wickham Common

Distance	5.2 miles
Approximate time	Two and a half hours
Start and finish	The Kings Head public house in Wickham Square, 4 miles north of Fareham reached via the A32. There is metered parking in The Square at Wickham. The better option is at the end of Station Road and along Mill Lane where two community association sponsored free car parks are provided. Grid reference 573115
Refreshments	Cafes, tea rooms and pubs in Wickham Square
Map	OS 1:25,000 Explorer Sheet 119 Meon Valley

Easy walking on mainly well established paths, including the Meon Valley Trail and the Pilgrim's Trail. There are no significant gradients or physical hazards. Care with route finding is needed in the wooded area of West Walk. The busy A32 main road has to be crossed in two places and the B2177 once. Also, in the later stages of the walk, the route passes down 100 Acres Road for three quarters of a mile. This is a pleasant tree-lined road and is not a main through route. It is though, the main access road to West Walk car park and some private houses, and carries traffic to these places. There is no pavement but it is possible to walk on the verge, mainly on the left.

1. With your back to The Kings Head, go left across the square and turn right down Bridge Street following the sign 'The Chesapeake Mill'.

There are some old and very pretty cottages on this street. One on the right carries a fearsome 18th Century warning to vagrants! The Chesapeake Mill, now containing a tea room and fine interior decoration salesrooms, is probably the most famous building in Wickham. The mill has timbers in its structure from the former US Navy frigate Chesapeake. Note also the restored Dip Hole steps just in front of the mill. The people of Wickham used to collect their water here, in the days before piped supplies.

A warning for penniless walkers?
The old vagrancy sign in Bridge Street
in Wickham

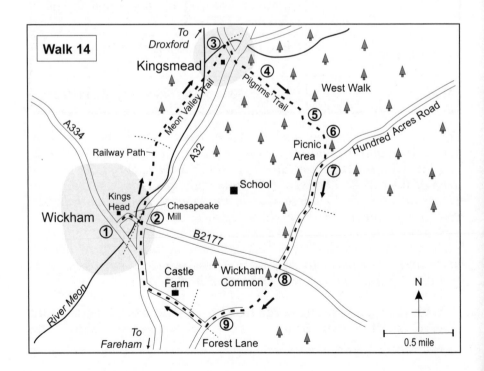

The Chesapeake Mill in Wickham

2. **Just beyond the mill, at the end of Bridge Street, go under the old railway bridge and take the steps on the right up to the top of the embankment.**

You can stand on the bridge here of the old Meon Valley Railway line to gain good views over the Wickham rooftops, the parish church of St Nicholas across the road, and the landscaped course of the River Meon below.

Walk north along the railway path, now a walkers route and bridleway. Shortly, on the left in the area where Wickham station used to be, you will see the 'Meon Valley Trail' sign that explains some interesting features of this route and a brief history of the railway. Initially, the river is on the left but you soon cross it. The first part of this stretch is in a wooded cutting. Soon you go under

a brick bridge and the countryside opens out. Just over a mile and a quarter from Wickham, the route crosses the Meon again. A hundred yards or so ahead you will see another brick bridge.

3. **Go under it and immediately turn up the rudimentary steps on the left to gain the metalled road at Kingsmead. Turn left here and walk the short distance down to The Roebuck Hotel.**

This is a popular pub with walkers and you may wish to take some refreshment here.

4. **With your back to The Roebuck cross the A32 (with care) and go a few yards left to enter the West Walk/Forest of Bere, at the finger post and sign reading 'Riding by Permit Only'.**
   About 50 yards into the wood, turn left by the signpost onto the Pilgrims Trail – see 'By the Way' at the end of the walk directions. This angles up through the wood in a generally south-easterly direction. The forest is quite dense here so you have to keep a keen eye for the waymark posts. After about 300 yards you come to a joining point with a broad track coming in from the left.

5. **Turn right here and at the crosstrack post reading 'West Walk 960 M', continue in this direction. The track is broad and the forest is now cleared to the right.**

6. **Turn right at the 'Car Park' direction sign and follow the broad track as it ascends for about 250 yards to the West Walk car park and picnic area. It should have taken you about 15 minutes to reach this point from The Roebuck.**

West Walk car park and picnic area is extensive and well-laid out. There are toilets, picnic tables and barbecue sites. There is a new and delightful children's playground. Roughly modelled on a North American 'frontier post' of the colonial period, there are log cabins, tepees, swings, sand pits and climbing nets in the trees for the children to enjoy in safety. There are other signposted short walks from this location also.

7. **Leave West Walk by the main entrance gate on 100 Acres Road and turn right.**

The actual gazetted footpath follows this road for half its length. However, there is no pavement and the road can be busy as it is the main access route into West Walk. There are verges on both sides of the road and you should walk on these. The verge on the left offers the safest possibility. 100 Acres Road is quite straight and you can see oncoming traffic clearly after you have rounded the bend at the top. Walk carefully down this road for three quarters of a mile. It should take about fifteen minutes, to the B2177.

8. Cross the B2177, here following the line of a Roman Road, and follow the finger post onto the broad and pot-holed dirt road, that is the entrance-way into Wickham Common.

   Some 150 yards from the B2177, take an obvious but unsigned path on the right. It runs alongside a thick furze and gorse hedge, which you keep on the right as you progress across the open, grass slope.

There are good views away to the east here towards Southwick.

Pass under the very conspicuous power lines and veer to the right to reach the top-end end of Forest Lane.

9. Turn right onto the lane and walk for about five minutes. Beyond the green 'Wickham Common' sign, after the houses on the left, watch out for a finger post on the right. Turn right here onto a 'Green Lane' that leads down to pass Castle Farm and between fields to the A32. You again have to cross this busy main road to get to the pedestrian walkway on the other side. Turn right and walk down into Wickham. Enter the village, just under the old railway bridge, and The Square is a few yards ahead.

By the Way

Chesapeake and Shannon

The United Sates Navy frigate Chesapeake was involved in a famous and ferocious naval battle with the 36 gun Royal Navy frigate HMS Shannon in the western Altantic ocean off the coast of Boston, Massachusetts, on 1 June 1813. The naval action was one of the defining events of the Anglo-American War of 1812. Both Captain Philip Broke of the Shannon and Captain James Lawrence of the Chesapeake became national heroes in their respective countries. Broke for his personal heroism in leading the cutlass-wielding boarding party onto Chesapeake where he was grievously wounded; and Lawrence for his cry 'don't give up the ship' as he lay dying, felled by an RN sharpshooter's musket shot. This utterance has been the wartime rallying cry for the United States Navy ever since. After the battle the Chesapeake was taken into Halifax, Nova Scotia, as a British 'prize'. She was later refitted and taken into Royal Navy service as HMS Chesapeake.

She served for several more years and was then taken into Portsmouth and broken up in 1820. Some of her timbers were purchased for use in the mill at Wickham.

The Pilgrims Trail

Not to be confused with the Pilgrims Way along the North Downs to Canterbury, the Pilgrims Trail in Hampshire recreates a medieval route used by a group called the 'Miquelots' from the shrine of St Swithun at Winchester Cathedral through Bishops Waltham and Portsmouth and over the Channel to Mont St Michel in Normandy. This long distance footpath, a short stretch of which is utilised here and also in Walk 18, is unique being waymarked in both England and France. A form of walkers' spiritually-codified 'entente cordiale' if you like. There was widespread devotion, some say cultish obsession, to Saint Michael throughout Britain from the 9th century.With many churches still carrying his name, Michaelmas, St Michael's Day, occurs on 29 September. Some devotees choose to walk on sections of the Pilgrim's Trail on that day.

15: To the 'end of the line via an English vineyard: A short 'I Spy and Tell' ramble

Millennium Green – Twenty questions – Vineyards

Distance	3-3.5 miles
Approximate time	Two hours
Start and finish	Wickham Water Meadows Millennium Green, Winchester Road, Wickham. Grid reference 572112
Refreshments	See Walk 14. The Wickham Water Meadows Millennium Green is a fine place for a picnic
Map	OS 1:25,000 Explorer Sheet 119 Meon Valley

This is an easy and short stroll on level ground and making use of the railway path. It is a good walk to do with active children. The walk provides a close-up look at an English vineyard. A watch has to be kept for flying golf balls in the crossing of Wickham Golf Course.

This is a fun walk and answers to 'I Spy' questions are sought along the route to the picturesque Webbs Land Vineyard, one of several in this part of Hampshire. The route passes on beyond the vineyard to the north end of the Meon railway path that finishes at a metal fence below Knowle Village. The MVR line used to join the still-operational Fareham-Eastleigh main line at this point.

To liven up the walk there are 20 questions to answer. An eagle-eye is needed to spot the clues, objects and landscape features that will give the answers to the questions. Some are open to discussion! If there are four people or more in the party, the group may divide into teams to see who can get the answers first. Don't forget to carry a piece of paper or notebook and pencil to write down the answers. Good luck!

(Answers at the end of the book.)

1. **Go into the Wickham Water Meadows Millennium Green on Winchester Road. Follow the path to the picturesque wooden bridge and seating area by the sluice and mill race in the river.**

   Q1. What kinds of birds are named on the 'Welcome to Wickham Water Meadows' sign fronting Winchester Road?
   Q2. Which public house contributed a bench to the seating area by the bridge?
   Q3. What word completes this phrase on the green manufacturing plate on the smaller bridge .... Hardwood Structures?

2. **Now walk the few yards up to Wickham Square and cross Winchester Road at the traffic lights. Go left and then right into Tanfield Lane and walk ahead with the open ground of the golf course on your right.**

   At the end of Tanfield Lane by the fingerpost, search for a partly-hidden small metal post below the tall conifers.

The Walk 15 quiz starts here in the Wickham Water Meadows Millennium Green

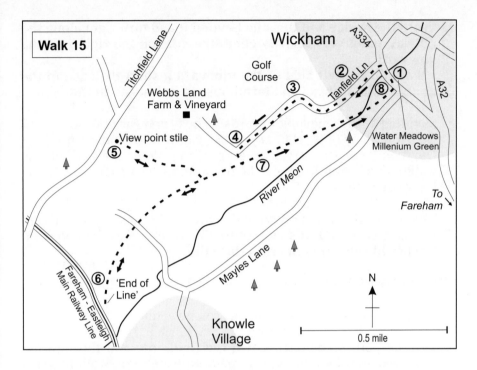

Q4. What is the capital letter on this post?

3. **Turn right with the fingerpost and walk up the track to the next turn.**

Q5. How many red/orange lifebuoys can you see at the first pond on the right?

At these ponds, the route turns left. Go ahead on the concrete track to the first waymarked post on the left.

Q6. What kind of man-made 'hole' in the ground is just a few yards to the left?

Continue ahead until you come to the small wooden foot bridge over the stream.

Q7. What do the two brick pillars support?

4. Cross the bridge and the stile beyond it and turn right along the railway path. Very shortly climb the stile on the right into the vineyard.
   Walk up the left side of the vineyard a short distance to the double stile. Webbs Land farmhouse is just ahead to the right.

Standing at the stile look towards Webbs Land Farmhouse.
Q8. How many of its chimney stacks can you see and count?
Q9. What are the larger trees growing along the line of the watercourse here? Clues can be found in the leaf shape and in the litter below the trees.

Now cross the stile and go half-right up the field to the stile in the corner that leads out onto the farm access track from Titchfield Lane. Do not cross this stile.

Stop here and sit for a while. With your back to the stile look across the Meon Valley.
Q10. How many electricity pylons can be counted?

5. Retrace your steps back down the field, into and through the vineyard, to rejoin the railway path. Now go right. Walk forward and you will reach an old railway bridge which you pass under.

About 150-200 yards beyond the bridge, look for silver birch and other trees by the pylon growing to the left and right beside the track. Q11.What is colonizing several of the tree trunks here?

Continue to the 'end of the line' at the iron fence where the main line from Eastleigh converges on the right. Find a gap in the trees by the moss covered sleeper to look across the river to the left.

Q12.What crowns the roofline of the two once prominent public buildings in Knowle Village?

6. Now return the way you came along the railway path. At the stile you crossed earlier from the golf course, by the wooden bridge, keep straight ahead on the railway path.

Q13 What is the purpose of the Southern Water installation by the

river on the right? After answering this question look behind you.
Q14. What does the signpost reveal is the name of the railway junction you have just returned from?

7. **Continue ahead on the railway path, now blue bridleway signed, to the vicinity of Mayles Farm.**

A large house in landscaped water gardens can be seen on the right.
Q15. What colour is it painted ?
Now stand on the bridge.
Q16. What man-made contrivances shape the channel of the River Meon here?

Continue ahead to the start of the wire fence on the right and look down the embankment into the wooded wetlands to the left.

Q17. What is the large tree completely circled by?

You now come to an old viaduct that once carried the railway over the Meon river. Look over the parapet on the right.

Q18. How many wooden footbridges cross the Meon from back gardens?

A little further, at the end of the wire fence, look down the embankment through the trees to the right.
Q19. What is the name on the street sign opposite?

8. **As you reach Wickham, you will cross the old bridge over Winchester Road. About 150 yards further on complete the walk by descending the embankment into the Water Meadows Millennium Green on the left.**

Q20. How many steps make-up this wood and gravel stairway?

By the Way

Hampshire Vineyards

There are something like 400 vineyards in the UK, almost all of them in the south of England and in one or two southern parts of Wales. Most are small being seldom larger than 5 acres. The largest in the country is Denbies Wine Estate which has 265 acres of vines at Dorking in the Mole Valley of Surrey. Wine production in this country is now a burgeoning industry. Some people say this is due to climate warming making grape cultivation more feasible. Maybe! However, the Romans grew grapes on the Isle of Wight 2000 years ago. A more likely driver of the industry is growing interest amongst the British public in organic and natural food and drink production. This, coupled with the development of post World War II continental-style wine drinking habits at mealtimes, has also led to a growing niche market, particularly for good white wines. Improvements in wine production technology and the adaptation of grape varieties suitable to soil and climate conditions in the southern part of England have helped. Hampshire vineyards feature wines made from such grape varieties as Reichensteiner, Rondo, Seyval and Champagne derivatives such as Pinot Noir and Chardonnay. Vineyards are usually accessible by appointment only. However, just a mile or two from the start of this walk on the road to Botley, is the commercial Wickham Vineyard. This welcomes visitors for tours and tastings, there is a bottle shop for purchases, an award-winning restaurant, an informative video presentation on the techniques of wine production, and a 7.5 hectare nature reserve on the estate. Wandering round the latter after a tasting can be a pleasant addition to Walk 15.

See www.wickhamvineyard.com Ph 01329 834042.

16: An echo of the Battle of Britain near Fareham's 'unknown river' on the way to Fiddlers Green

Unknown river – Battle of Britain – Garden village

Distance	8.5 miles
Approximate time	Four hours
Start and finish	Wallington Village Hall on Broadcut just north of the High Street in Fareham. The Broadcut car park in front of the village hall is free at the weekends but waiting time Monday-Friday is 3 hours. The long-stay, pay and display Lysses car park is behind the High Street in Fareham. It is free on Sundays and Bank Holidays. This is close to the walk start which is reached via a footbridge over Wallington Way. Grid reference 583066
Refreshments	All the facilities of Fareham town centre are within ten minutes walk of the start point
Map	OS 1:25,000 explorer Sheet 119 Meon Valley

This is a fairly long walk but there are no significant gradients or difficulties and much of the route uses well-waymarked and broad farm tracks. The walk is one of pleasant surprises. You start amidst the hustle and bustle of a thriving town, Fareham, but within a few minutes of the start you pass under the M27 motorway and enter an area of quiet countryside and mixed farmland along the course of the Wallington River. This attractive, often sparkling stream, is a junior cousin of the Meon and sometimes described as 'Fareham's unknown river'. The later sections of the walk include the pleasant woodlands of

Fiddlers Green that rise above the east bank of the Meon and the open fields that surround the newly landscaped Knowle Village. The early part of the walk, across the fields beside the Wallington River, can be wet and subject to local flooding around the stiles after heavy rain in winter. I would recommend reserving this walk for the drier months of spring and summer.

1. **Behind Wallington Village Hall take the footpath along the left bank of the Wallington River.**

   Cross a wooden footbridge and, keeping the river on the right, go ahead through a part open, part-wooded area to reach a yellow waymarked gate by the road (Standard Way) that leads into the Wallington trading estate. Cross the road and take the underpass that carries the Wallington River under the M27. Emerge to follow the waymarks that lead you around the left edge of a field to a substantial footbridge over the weir. Cross this and go across the field at an angle to the stile into the lane (Spurlings Road).

The poignant memorial to Flying Officer James Tillett R.A.F in Pook Lane

2. **Cross the stile and turn left along the road to quickly reach Pook Lane.**

You might like to stop here for a few moments contemplation by the small memorial. It reads: "F/O James Tillett 33454. RAF 238 Sqn. K.I.A. Nov 6 1940. Near to this memorial". There is also on the stone a short, moving poem by Graham Alderson, commemorating the young airman who gave his life for his country at this place in the later stages of the Battle of Britain.

3. **Continue ahead in the direction indicated by the fingerpost to pass the farm buildings. Go through the metal five bar gate at the farmhouse. It is an important one, so do please remember to close it behind you. Follow the concrete path ahead with fields sloping up to the right.**

4. **Shortly after the end of the concrete, cross the stile on the left and continue ahead now with a hedge on your right. Progress ahead through the fields and over the stiles alongside the Wallington River.**

Everything seems remote, rural, and scenic with Whitedell Farm up on the right completing the image of tranquil rusticity. All the more astonishing then, to pause and look back over your shoulder to see the modern tower of Fareham Civic Offices, a symbol of urban civilisation and authority (!!) looming and omnipresent not much more than a mile away. Just the type of thing that walkers like to get away from!

5. **Where the hedge 'kinks' right, go left at the waymarks to cross the footbridge over the river. Go right at first along the river bank and then veer left upto the edge of Pigeonhouse Copse.**
   Join the gravel track and walk up to Bere Farm. Pass a prominent 'three-way' fingerpost and in a further 100 yards or so, just beyond the farm buildings, turn left. The track now ascends gradually, equidistant between Orchard Copse (right) and Homerhill Copse (left).

Southward prospects from this track, in the vicinity of the lone birch tree, reveal the original Nelson's column (see 'By the Way' at the end of the walk directions) on Portsdown Hill and the ultra modern radar research installations further to the east.

6. **Progress straight ahead over two cultivated fields. As you approach the top of the upper field, where onward progress is stopped at a low bushy embankment, turn right for a few yards.**

Here, hidden behind a tree in the hedge, you will find a benefactor's memorial fingerpost carrying the footpath numbers '103, 104, 9, 9' and erected by the Meon Group of the Ramblers Association in 1981.

Cross the stile and keep ahead over the short field and go along a short, canopied, conifer drive to Forest Lane. The high ground

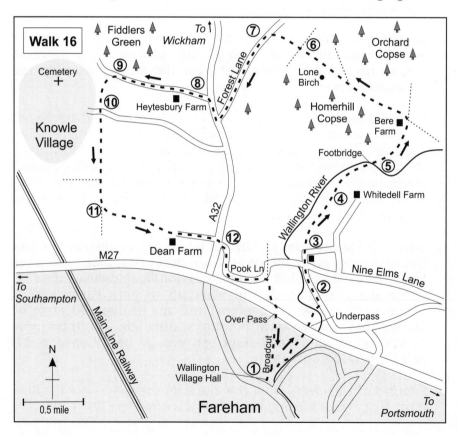

here acts as the watershed between the Meon (west) and Wallington (east) rivers.

7. Turn left and follow Forest Lane down to its junction with the A32. Cross the A323 with great care as it is an extremely busy road and this is a particularly fast section. Cross by the bus stop a few yards up on the right.

8. Turn almost immediately left into the yellow waymarked and separately signed 'Heytesbury Farm' track. Bypass the gate to walk between farm buildings. Continue ahead on the broad, concrete track as far as an open barn on the right. Keep ahead with the woodland of Fiddlers Green now on the right.

9. As you reach and progress into the left-hand corner of the woods, look for the easily missed, yard-high signpost with yellow waymarks.

   The mark signing the route you should follow is on the reverse of the post, out of your initial line of sight. Go left here down into a woody hollow and across a small rivulet that feeds the Meon. Go up the other side to the fence line around Knowle Village and hospital grounds. Keep to the path on the left side of the fence until you reach Knowle Road.

Go right if you wish to visit the village, take refreshment and view the interesting juxtaposition of Victorian and early 21st century domestic architecture. The woodland cemetery is worth a visit also.

10. Cross Knowle Road at the entrance to the village and keep ahead. You now enter an area of very large fields that stretch all the way down (southerly) to the M27. The track follows the right hand edge of the fields alongside the trees.

The high-rise skyline of Portsmouth with its prominent Spinnaker Tower can be seen off to the south-east.

About two thirds of the way down these fields, pass the waymark post on the right.

11. In a further 275 yards turn left at the cross tracks, alongside a

hedge. Go straight ahead towards the 'Cash and Carry' barns at Dean Farm.

There is much commercial activity on the large Dean Farm Estate and as you approach the barns it is important to follow the clear footpath indicators which direct you slightly to the right away from the barn access road. Look out for the beautifully restored farmhouse and original timber barn on your right.

12. **Continue to the A32 and cross it once again. Go down Pook Lane. This has a walkable grass verge, initially on the left and, once round the bend, on the right. Pook Lane carries local traffic but is not busy compared to the M27 immediately to your right! At North Fareham Farm, turn right onto the narrow path which is actually blue-signed as a bridleway. Presumably it is to be used by 'narrow' horses and riders only! Go left and right over the arched concrete bridge over the motorway. Descend to the tree-lined path that keeps the trading estate on the left to exit at Broadcut. Wallington Village hall is just 250 yards ahead past the industrial units on the left.**

By the Way

Nelson's column

A fact unknown to many Britons is that there are at least three 'Nelson's Columns'.

There is the famous one in London's Trafalgar Square, another one at the extremity of the harbour jetty in Great Yarmouth, and this one on top of Portsdown Hill overlooking Portsmouth Harbour. More correctly termed 'Nelson's Monument', it was paid for largely out of Royal Navy funds and erected in 1807. It thus predates its Trafalgar Square rival which was completed in 1843. Inscriptions on the Monument describe the Battle of Trafalgar. Adjacent to the memorial is the Palmerstonian Fort Nelson, now one of the museums of the Royal Armouries with an extensive collection of naval ordnance and militaria.

Knowle Village

This is a contemporary residential development in a rural setting on the eastern slope of the lower Meon river valley. It is based upon and makes use of many of the retained buildings of the former Knowle Hospital, a large psychiatric institution that opened in a farmland setting in 1852. Originally known as the Hampshire County Lunatic Asylum, it came to have the same compact and self-contained character of many of the large Victorian mental hospitals built as national policy under the 1845 County Asylums and Lunacy Act. These were often dispersed to out-of-the way rural locations in the English counties. Constructed of local Hampshire red bricks, much of the building work was undertaken by Russian prisoners-of-war from the Crimean war.

The hospital came to acquire many of the functions associated with psychiatric care and in the 1950s it catered for more than 2000 patients. At one time, it had its own farm, craft shops, kitchens and bakeries, and its own halt on the Meon valley railway. The graves of 5578 former patients, hospital estate residents and staff are in its two acre, somewhat overgrown, woodland cemetery. The burials commenced in 1852 and ceased in 1971. The cemetery is below the village on the northern side and it is still consecrated ground though maintained as a local 'nature reserve'. The hospital finally closed in 1996 though a secure residential accommodation block for psychiatric patients remains in the Ravenswood facility on the edge of the village.

The new development with a range of housing provision is an interesting example of modern 'garden-town' planning; for Knowle Village almost is a small town in its own right. The village remains surrounded by fields and woods and the inner part has landscaped courtyards and squares, often eerily quiet and seemingly deserted on weekdays. There has been considerable tree planting and the creation of public open spaces. The chapel has been restored for general community use, and the former main administration building with its original clock tower, is at the centre of the development backing onto a pedestrianised community square with shops and a café. Several of the old ward blocks, though converted to up-market apartments, still retain their institutional appearance and it is a telling and atmospheric experience to walk around and among them.

17: Funtley: circling the site of a pioneer ironmaster's foundry

Ironmaster Henry Cort – Millennium sculptures – Westbury Manor Museum

Distance	5 miles
Approximate time	Two and a half hours
Start and finish	At The Deviation Line car park and recreation ground on Highlands Road, about one and a half miles north west of Fareham town centre. The car park is free but bollard controlled and access may be restricted. Grid reference 557072
Refreshments	Fareham town centre shops, pubs and cafes. Highlands Road shopping centre, which has food outlets, is adjacent the start of the walk
Map	OS 1:25,000 Explorer Sheet 119 Meon Valley

The walk starts at the Deviation Line recreation space in Fareham (see 'By the Way' at the end of the walk description). The walk is easy with no gradients, though link paths on the sides of the railway embankment can be slippery in wet weather. The route is generally well signed though you have to look closely for the waymarks around the iron foundry site, farm buildings, and upstream when you re-cross the Meon. Stiles and gates are mainly easy to negotiate. The paddocks to be crossed are usually well-grassed and the paths follow the edges of these away from horses and livestock.

1. Walk ahead through the old railway cutting of the Meon Valley railway.

This is a pleasant area of public land now set aside for recreation. The wooded sides of the cutting (which tend to hide the houses at the top on each side) create an illusion of already being in open countryside. That has to wait for 10 minutes more, until you have gone through the underpass of the M27.

2. **On exiting the underpass, turn immediately left on to the way-marked path that runs alongside the M27 for 100 metres or so.**
   The path turns right and, as it descends towards farm buildings, becomes more track-like. Veer left (there is another path down to the right but ignore it) to reach a bare metal stile by a house. Turn right and in a few metres left at the waymark post, opposite the barns. This brings you down to a bridge over the Meon River.

In the fields to the right, was the site of Henry Cort's iron foundry. Here, he perfected the 'puddling' techniques to produce wrought iron of a quality that captured the attention of the Royal Navy and producers of iron goods. The techniques developed here reduced Britain's dependency on imported wrought iron of superior quality from Russia and Sweden. Cort's techniques were taken up in iron foundries all over Britain – just in time for the Napoleonic wars.

There is very little visible evidence now of this cradle of the Industrial Revolution. Two clearly engineered channels of the river meet at the bridge. There is a sign reading 'Ironmasters House' on the outbuilding just over the bridge. To the left is the brickwork of a mill race once used to power the waterwheels of the foundry.The irregularities and tussock mounds in the fields are the only outward signs of a unique but long gone industrial enterprise. Now the land has returned to agricultural use and the only 'noise' of industry comes from the traffic on the nearby M27.

3. **Cross the bridge and ascend the track for about 50 yards to find a finger post pointing acutely to the right.**
   Follow this path to cross a paddock via stiles in the direction of a very striking line of tall conifers that lead up to a splendidly sited large house up to the left. Pass by the end of this conifer line and take the path through the yard of a market garden company. You will come very shortly to a footpath sign by a metal gate.

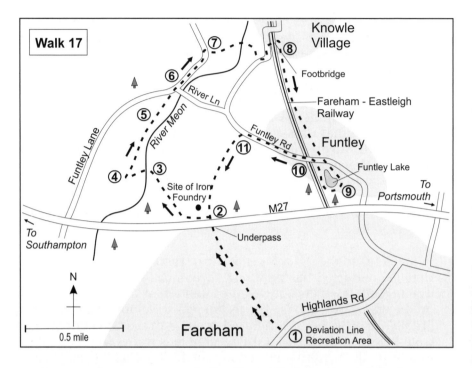

4. **Cross at the gate to reach the first stile into the paddocks.**

Pause here to take in the good views over the river, the fishponds created from the overflow channels, and the site of the foundry back over your right shoulder on the far bank. Note the picnic table on a gravel spit just in the channel of the river. Nice place in summer to keep the feet cool in the water whilst taking a picnic. Sadly, this facility is on private land and is out of bounds to walkers.

5. **The path now follows the right hand edge of several fields or paddocks. At my count, there were five stiles and three new wooden gates to negotiate. Come out onto River Lane by the bridge. Keep alert as there is a surprising amount of traffic taking a short cut into Funtley via this minor road.**

The riverbanks and meadows hereabouts are owned by the worthy Second Chance childrens charity. Children from difficult backgrounds have the opportunity here to learn about farming, conservation and rural traditions. Perhaps some even go on to take up farming in adult life.

6. **At River Lane turn left and immediately right onto the main road signed 'Wickham 3. Shedfield 2'.**

   Be mindful of traffic and take care as you walk on the right hand grass verge for about 250 metres to the 'Danger Tractors Turning' sign. Note the fingerpost and turn right through the walker's gate onto the farm track.

7. **Walk down to and walk across the footbridge over the Meon.**

   People have been known to panic here! It looks as though you are walking right into the front garden of an idyllic cottage by the river. Well, the house, grounds and riverbank are certainly private. However a small sign on the footbridge tells you that you are welcome to walk this way. Very reassuring!

   As you cross this wooden footbridge note the pretty 'Island in the Stream' to the left, complete with its own developed patch of bamboo! Climb the path up through the wood to emerge on the road that leads to the rear of the former Knowle psychiatric hospital.

8. **Turn left and walk up the road to the bend – about 50 yards – where a sign on the right directs you to use the footbridge over the operational Fareham-Eastleigh railway line. Cross this bridge and turn right at the far end on a path between a barbed wire fence on the left and a lattice metal fence on the right.**

   Soon, fields open out to the left with views towards Portsdown Hill. Some six minutes walking from the railway footbridge brings you to a stile in front of houses. Go over it and pass between houses to reach Funtley Lane.

9. **Turn left and in 50 yards reach The Miners Arms pub in Funtley village.**

   You may want to take some refreshment here.

   From the pub, cross Funtley Road and pass over the grass strip between the houses to reach the edge of Funtley Lake.

Popular with locals and anglers, this pretty reed and willow fringed lake has a good path and boardwalk (in the wetter places) going right around it. Do the circuit from left to right. On a fine day this is a nice place to picnic, or just to loiter for a while to watch the water birds.

10. Back at Funtley Road, turn left and walk up and over the railway bridge. As the road curves to the right, a further disused railway bridge comes into sight about 300 metres ahead. Make for this but do take care as you have to walk half of this section on the grass verge.

11. Go under the old railway bridge and immediately turn up left on a short path to the top of the embankment.

You are now back on the lower valley section of the railway path, the Deviation Line route of the Meon Valley railway. This section has been turned into a bridle path and walkway.

The Deviation Line recreation area in Fareham: start and finish for Walk 17

Turn right and follow the railway path along the embankment through Hothouse Coppice. The Cort foundry site is now down to your right. Soon you regain the outward route at the M27 underpass. Go under the motorway one more and it is now a short walk back to the starting point.

By the Way

The Deviation Line
The Deviation Line was a loop on the Meon Valley Railway constructed to provide an alternative line into Fareham Station. It bypassed the Fareham tunnel which in its early years experienced structural problems. Similarly, trains using the deviation could continue without being delayed by shunting activity taking place in the sidings at Knowle and around an abattoir at Funtley.

The Henry Cort Millennium sculpture exhibition
This is in the pedestrianized area of West Street in the centre of Fareham. The permanent street sculptures here pay tribute to the work of Henry Cort via an unusual array of wrought iron, steel, wood and stone creations handmade in forges using traditional blacksmithing techniques. Also in West Street, in front of the Bus Station, is the Westbury Manor Museum set in a fine Georgian mansion in a fully landscaped garden. This contains exhibitions on life in Fareham and the Meon Valley area in former times with an emphasis on the social and economic history of the town and district and its once important local industries such as brewing and brickmaking. For interested visitors unfamiliar with or new to the area, the museum is a very useful first point of reference. Admission is free and the museum opens 10-5 pm Monday to Friday and 10-4 pm on Saturdays. **www.hants.gov.uk/westbury-manor-museum** Ph 0845 603 5635

18: Springs, moors, fens, Romans and brickmakers: the watershed at Swanmore and Bishops Waltham

Bishops Waltham Palace – Roman Road – Natural springs

Distance	10.8 miles
Approximate time	Five hours
Start and finish	The car park in Church Road, Swanmore, opposite St Barnabas parish church. Swanmore can be reached by forking right off the A334 at Shedfield Common, approximately one and a half miles beyond Wickham. Grid reference 576164
Refreshments	Two pubs, the New Inn and the Rising Sun are close to the start of the walk at Swanmore. Bishops Waltham with a full range of convenience stores, cafes and tea rooms, public toilets and a gem of a 16th Century inn, The Crown, is visited twice on the walk
Map	OS 1:25,000 Explorer Sheet 119 Meon Valley

At more than ten miles this is the longest walk in the book and takes in four local nature reserves and several sites of interest to the archeologist and the student of natural history. If you want to spend time exploring the impressive ruins of the Bishops Palace at Bishops Waltham, a worthwhile activity that I would recommend, you probably need to make this a full day walk. There are no gradients to speak of on this walk. The route crosses the watershed from the edge of the Meon Valley near Swanmore, to the headstream sources of the Hamble river around Bishops Waltham. Geologically, the walk is located in the junction areas of the Cretaceous chalk and the clays and gravels of the Reading Beds. The impervious nature of the clays means that many natural springs well up in this area. Indeed, the later part of this walk is excellent for examining spring hydrology at close quarters. The downside of this is that some of the paths can be very wet in winter as the water table is very close to the surface. Boots, preferably waterproof, are recommended for this walk.

If the planned distance seems too long, then you can reduce the length of the walk by three miles by stopping at Bishops Waltham and picking up the return route in the town centre car park in Red Lion Street. You will however, miss out on two of the nature reserves if you exercise this option.

1. **From the car park turn left along Church road and right into New Road at the post office, opposite the church. Turn left into Chapel Road to pass The New Inn which does home cooked food and has a beer garden. Walk down to the cross roads.**

   The Rising Sun pub is just on the left. At the cross roads turn right with the sign 'Shedfield 2'. In about 350 yards, at the '30' sign, turn right onto a gravel lane.

   This is actually an 'unadopted' road called The Lakes. It is presumably named for the small ponds which dot the fields either side here and which drain into the stream on the left.

   Cross the stream at Belmont farm and continue ahead to New Road.

2. **Cross to the yellow waymarked gate opposite in front of the pylon. Continue to the end of the field. At the footbridge over the stream turn left and then right between houses to reach Lower Chase Road.**

   There is an unusual white timberboard cottage with a corrugated iron roof here.

   Turn left along the lane, which can be busy, and walk up to the B2177. Turn right and walk on the pavement a few hundred yards up to The Chase Inn, which proclaims itself the 'Waltham Chase gastro pub'. Cross the road at the bus stop just past the pub.

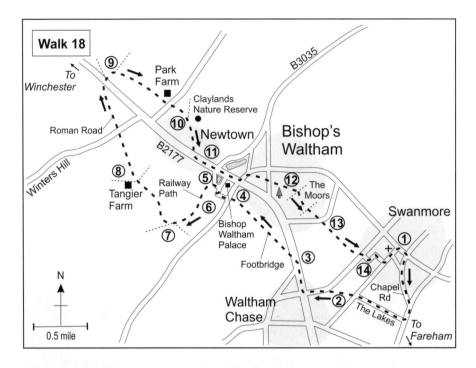

3. **From the waymarked fingerpost continue ahead along the right edge of the fields as the path begins to swing in a north-westerly direction.**

   Cross the footbridge over the stream and continue straight ahead. You then reach another footbridge over one of the two headstreams of the Hamble river. Veer right to pass two upended sections of railway line acting as a stile in the fence line. Progress up the right hand side of pleasant fields to the top of the slope. Then down to the metal fingerpost at the field exit to the road.

4. **Cross this road and, just to the left, go down the lane alongside the high boundary wall of the Bishops Waltham Palace.**

   As you go round the corner at the bottom at Palace House, the ruins come starkly into full view. If you wish to visit the site continue up to the main road and go right for the entrance. There is also a convenience store across the road here. And the centre of Bishops Waltham is close to hand.

5. **To continue the walk from the palace, go to the left around the attractive Bishops Waltham town pond.**

The site of the old mill on the leftis earmarked controversially for a Sainsbury's supermarket.

Just past the end of this site are the still extant level crossing gates of the abandoned Botley-Bishops Waltham branch railway line. It closed in 1962 and this part of the line is now a local nature reserve. The sign here is 'Pilgrims Trail. Winchester 11.8 miles'.

6. **Follow this railway path for just over half a mile.**

Very pleasant it is too, well-wooded and with rustic benches to rest upon. It is also a great place for bird watchers. Reported sightings amongst many here include treecreepers, blackcaps, green and great spotted woodpeckers, chiffchaffs and goldcrests. At dusk,

The ruins of the once magnificent Bishops Waltham Palace: 'slighted' in the English Civil war

tawny and little owls can be heard hooting and bats apparently feed in the hedgerows on either side of the old railway path.

7. **Leave the railway path at the wooden gate and go half-right along the lane. In a few yards, at the fingerpost by the metal gate, turn acutely down to the right to cross the stream.**

    Swing left to immediately pass a pylon. Follow the waymarks as the path hugs the stream on the left. Soon cross two adjacent waymarked stiles to turn along the right bank of the stream (avoid the temptation to cross the rudimentary footbridge in front of you here). Keep close to the right bank of the stream through fields to a gate into the lane below Tangier Farm.

8. **Cross the lane (and stream) slightly to the left, to go through another gate and across a field to a stile. Do not cross this stile. Instead, swing right and half-right again with the waymark to re-cross the stream at the wooden bridge.**

    Cross a double stile and pass to the left of the nursery sheds. You now go ahead through fields with stiles and ditches to eventually come through a tussock grass field to a lane.

On the Pilgrims Trail. An abandoned level crossing gate is the entrance to the nature reserve at Bishops Waltham

Cross the lane to the waymarked access track also signed 'Winters Hill farm'. Walk ahead to take the clearly signed path around the farm buildings to the right. Rejoin the farm track which is actually the line of the ancient Roman Road from Winchester to Portchester on the upper reaches of Portsmouth harbour.

9. Arriving at the B2177, cross to the lane opposite and walk up it for 100 yards.

   You now leave the Pilgrim's Trail, which is signed in front of you. Instead, turn acutely right over the fingerposted stile and pass around the edge of the field. In front of the ponds, cross the stile on the right and go straight ahead across open fields. Cross a stile into a fenced path to exit into a lane at Park Dairy farm. Cross the stile on the other side of the lane with barns on the right. More fields and stiles follow until you reach a gate with a sign reading 'Claylands Local Nature Reserve'.

10. Enter the nature reserve occupying former clay pits that actually date from Roman times and which gave rise to an important tile and brick making industry here in the 19th century.

This is a high point and you can see out over Bishops Waltham. There is an informative signboard relating how bricks and terracotta pots from here were transported along the Bishops Waltham branch line to be eventually incorporated into the structure of Buckingham Palace, the Victoria and Albert Museum, and other notable building around the country. Production finally ceased in 1956.

11. Go to the right to the exit gate of the reserve, and go left down the field to the fingerpost and out to the main road. Turn left to walk down into Bishops Waltham.

As you go, look out for the '1865' date on the workers cottages opposite the Priory Inn. The cottages have the unmistakeable, architectural character of an industrial estate of the late Victorian period. They were built for the workers in the brick industry and gave rise to an estate development here called 'Newtown'.

Bishops Waltham is an attractive small town and it is worth a half hour or so of exploration. To commence the final section of the walk, find your way to the main car park in Red Lion Street.

12. **With your back to the Bishops Waltham Social Club go up to the United Free Church to walk along Little Shore Lane. At its end turn right and second left into Cricklemede. At the bend cross the road to enter the 'Moors Local Nature Reserve.'**

Go to the right for about 200 yards into the trees to find and view the very unusual Sand Boils. These are constant mini eruptions of spring water in gravel beds that act as a source for the Hamble river.

Retrace your steps and cross the field to the right (or left from the Moors entrance gate) to pass over two small plank bridges to the trees. Go through the gate to pass through the woods. At the next gate go half-right past a bench to a signboard reading 'Wildlife at the Fen'.

This explains how the many springs that reach the surface here create unique fen-style forms of vegetation requiring special land management techniques.

13. **Go to the left of the fen signboard to leave the Moors at the exit gate. Immediately pass through another gate and go straight ahead on a fenced path.**
    Go through a gate into a small field to go to the right round yet another spring pond. This one can be examined at close quarters. Pass through a coppice to an unusually long, log bridge at a lane.

14. **Cross the lane and go ahead at the 'Public Footpath' fingerpost. Wind through woods to come out onto Lower Chase Road. Cross the road to enter Marsh's Meadow just beyond the sign 'Public Footpath. Walkers Only'.**

This is the fourth and final local nature reserve.

Cross the meadow diagonally to the top gate. Go through it to the left to find the signboard by the pond.

This explains how Swanmore Conservation Group, on behalf of the Parish Council, maintain Marsh's Meadow and adjacent Green's Wood as important local nature reserves and public open spaces. The meadow is an important habitat for slowworms, the Burnet moth, black and yellow wasp spiders, caterpillars and common grasshoppers. Southern hawker dragonflies frequent the pond and newts and frogs live and spawn in it. Beside the pond turn left to find the entrance into Green's Wood.

Pass through the mainly ash, oak and yew woodland on the well-established, raised and timber-rimmed pathway. Exit at the Church Road gate. The car park where you started is a few yards along to the right. Perhaps more appetizingly and as a nice surprise at the end of this long walk, the Brickmakers pub is close on the left!.

By the Way

Bishops Waltham Palace
This is a Scheduled Ancient Monument under the control of English Heritage.

The ruins of the moated palace offer testimony to the power and wealth of the Bishops of Winchester. The original palace was built in 1135 by Henry De Blois, an aristocratic Norman related by line of descent to William the Conqueror and King Stephen. The palace was one of a series of great houses built within the diocese of Winchester for use by the clergy as they traveled about the countryside. Other similar functioning palaces included Farnham and Wolvesey castles. Henry was Bishop of Winchester from 1129 until his death in 1171. He was also Abbot of Glastonbury. The beneficiary of titles and estates in Normandy, his political power, wealth and influence enabled Winchester to rival, and for a time compete for church and political leadership with the bishops at Canterbury Cathedral. The wealth of Winchester allowed for many social and economic works to be undertaken including the digging of drainage ditches and the building of almshouses. Indeed Winchester was the richest diocese in England in the medieval period and held great sway at court. William Wykeham, the founder of Winchester College became bishop in 1367 and he made additions to the buildings. During the English Civil War the palace was besieged by the Parliamentarians and 'slighted' – a military euphemism for all but destroyed. It has remained a ruin, albeit a very impressive and romantic one, ever since.
www.ecastles.co.uk/waltham.html

19: Via the banks of the ancient Meon canal to the village of Titchfield

Meon canal – King Charles bridge – Titchfield Abbey

Distance	5.7 miles
Approximate time	Three hours
Start and finish	Titchfield Haven foreshore car park (western end) by Meon Road at Hillhead. 4 miles south of Titchfield via A27. Grid reference 531023
Refreshments	Titchfield Haven Visitor Centre café at the start/finish. Four pubs in Titchfield. Tea room in the garden centre adjacent to Titchfield Abbey
Map	OS 1:25,000 Explorer Sheet 119 Meon Valley

The first half of the walk is along the towpath of the ancient canalized section of the Meon river. The towpath is lined in places with shady attractive tree. This makes for easy walking with no gradients. However, some parts of the track alongside the canal section are prone to local flooding after heavy rain in winter. People often walk in Wellington boots here and they may be a viable option for winter walking. The return section of the walk is along an open, and well-defined trackway across farmland. This section is relatively high and provides fine views across the river valley and south to The Solent. The walk is particularly recommended for summer when the tracks are generally dry, the wayside and meadow flowers (which can be quite prolific here) are in full bloom, and cooling breezes from The Solent make for pleasant walking conditions.

1. Cross the road in front of the foreshore public conveniences at Titchfield Haven foreshore car park at Hillhead. Enter the Titchfield Haven Nature Reserve and take the path to the left. In just over 250 yards reach the Meon Marsh Sea Lock.

Signboards here explain how the 3rd Earl of Southampton canalized the Meon river in 1611. The 'staunch lock' as it was called, allowed vessels to enter the canal at high tide and sail as far as Titchfield where the earl had tanneries and other properties. The canal was needed because the Earl had dammed the river mouth closing it off from the sea. Apparently this was to create hay meadows and pasture land further upstream of the estuarine marshes. The canal had a short life and the Earl's grand commercial schemes were not fulfilled. Over the centuries the canal has become a pleasant, tree-girt and reed-fringed backwater.

2. **Walk north beside the canal on the broad and flat, but often muddy track.**

Titchfield Haven Nature Reserve is on the right and it is possible to spot some of the birds that frequent this internationally known sanctuary. These include lapwings, skylarks, wigeon from parts of Russia and black tailed godwits that migrate here from Iceland. Kingfishers may also be seen darting about the numerous channels and meres in the reserve. Ten minutes or so from the sea lock brings you to the brick arched Hammond Bridge (see 'By the Way' at the end of the walk description) on your left. Note it; for you will cross it on your return.

3. **Keep straight ahead with the canal always on the left.**

Parts of the watercourse flow within the banks at a level higher than the path being walked upon. This depends on the time of year and the rainfall. A half mile or so from Hammond Bridge join a bitumenized section of track.

Off to the right, on the valley slopes above the main channel of the Meon River, can be seen Hollam House. This was the site for the infamous 'duck house' that came to symbolize the scandal of MPs expenses in 2009...and the spectacular downfall of the Member for Gosport who lived here!!!!!

Continue north on the bitumen until it swings sharp left over the third brick bridge. Do not cross the bridge. Continue ahead beyond the stile on the grassy path. Soon reach the car park by the road entering Titchfield village.

4. **Cross the road and continue on the marked footpath, still alongside the canal.**

   In 100 yards or so, turn left to cross the canal, here almost at its end, on the ornate wooden footbridge. Follow the path adjacent to the churchyard wall of St Peter's. Turn right at the 'Skinhouse Piece' sign and walk through the serene, very English country churchyard, complete with magnificent yew trees. Leave the churchyard by taking the Church Path.

   Here, a row of cottages all have remarkably low, wooden front doors. Several of these, as elsewhere in Titchfield are painted blue, denoting estate origins.

5. **Turn left at East Street and pass The Wheatsheaf public house on the right. Turn left at the High Street, to enter The Square, the historic heart of Titchfield.**

   The village is worth exploring and there are signboards to read and fine buildings from different historic periods to view. Curious Sarsen Stones are to be found in West Street. They are halfway up this picturesque street from the elaborate nautical memorial claiming a '1000' years of port history for Titchfield in the small public garden in the corner of The Square. The well-preserved buildings of the former National School are towards the top of West Street. Two notable old ale houses confront each other across The Square, the Queens Head on the right and its competitor, The Bugle, on the left.

6. **Walk down South Street.**

   The oldest houses in Titchfield are here at Numbers 7 and 11. They were built originally in the 14th century to serve as storehouses for the monks of Titchfield Abbey. In 1961 during renovations, secret rooms were found in these ancient buildings.

7. **Turn right up Coach Hill and in 200 metres turn left into Lower Bellfield.**

   The Bellfield estate, a postwar urban housing construction, is not the architectural jewel in Titchfield's otherwise picturesque crown!

At the end of Lower Bellfield, cross Bellfield itself and take the short path opposite between the houses. It runs for a few yards with wooden fences on either side to come out on a grassy patch in front of garages.

8. Enter the field ahead by the waymarked steel cross-pole that passes for a gate. Annoyingly, you have to duck under this.

Go straight ahead (south) across the paddock to pass the next yellow waymark post with the trees and fenced property on your right. Go over the stile, cross the concrete farm track to cross another stile. Keep on the waymarked route along the left-hand side of this very large field. Note that some of the Hampshire County Council yellow waymarks in this section read 'Lower Meon Valley Trail'.

You are now on higher, open ground with the Meon Valley down to your left, the Isle of Wight in the distance, and the tower of Fawley Power Station at the end of Southampton Water, conspicuous to your right.

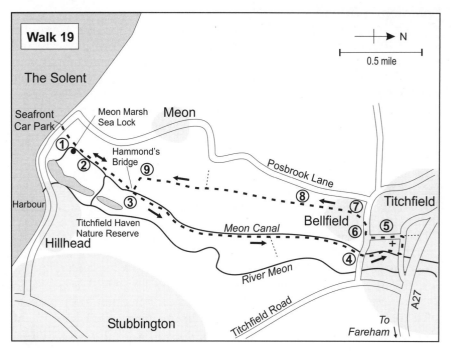

The track here crosses working farms and it is important to observe the waymarks and the various warning signs, especially those that ask for dogs to be kept on leads. After you have passed Posbrook Gardens Farm, the path develops into a paved farm track.

This is a fine, open and airy part of the walk with good views to every point of the compass.

After a mile or so or so from Bellfield, the track slopes downwards towards a wooded gully and turns sharp left. In 50 yards the track brings you to Hammond Bridge.

9. **Cross the bridge and turn right on to your outward route. It is about a 12 minute walk from here back to the Titchfield Haven foreshore car park.**

By the Way

Hammond's Bridge

If you like myths and legends this bridge is the one for you. A popular story is that Colonel Hammond, Governor of the Isle of Wight, arrested King Charles I in the vicinity during the hunt for the errant monarch in 1647. Some people like to believe the king was actually hiding under the bridge itself. If so,it wasn't this one. The current bridge is a brick, twin-arched low bridge of 19th century style and construction. It replaced an earlier 17th century structure when the canal fell into disuse.

Titchfield Abbey

You can extend this walk by continuing for half a mile north along the footpath that starts at the corner of East and High Streets in Titchfield. The route crosses the A27 behind the recreation ground and passes the restored 15th century and quite magnificent Tithe Barn.

Titchfield Abbey ruins remain starkly beautiful and powerfully evocative of a turbulent period in English history. This is probably the most historically significant building in the entire Meon Valley. It is a Scheduled Ancient Monument controlled by English Heritage who keep it and the high-walled garden surrounding it, open to the public.

The original abbey was built of stone from Dorset, the Isle of Wight and Caen in Normandy. It was consecrated in 1222 for an order of

The starkly impressive ruin of Titchfield Abbey. Established in 1222 for an order of Premonstratensian canons, the abbey was closed by Henry VIII in 1537

Premonstratensian canons also known as 'white canons' after the colour of their habits. Its full title was the Abbey Church of the Assumption of the Blessed Virgin. It enjoyed three centuries of monastic life, characterised by austerity in living, simple market gardening, devotion to scholarship, and the building up of an important ecclesiastical and sociopolitical library. In the monastic period, Richard the Second and Queen Anne stayed in 1393; Henry V was a guest on his way to Agincourt and everlasting glory in 1415; and in 1445 a royal wedding took place in the abbey church between Henry VI and Margaret of Anjou.

The abbey was closed under the orders of Henry VIII during the Dissolution of the Monasteries in 1537. A powerful courtier called Thomas Wriothesley, Earl of Southampton, coerced the abbott into selling the property and it was later converted into a fortified Tudor mansion that was given the name Place House. After generations of aristocratic ownership and visits by kings and queens including Edward VI, Elizabeth I, Charles I and Charles II, a prominent

Hampshire family called the Delmes purchased the property in 1741 and took up residence for 40 years. In 1781 for reasons that remain debated, they took a decision to demolish the building to create a 'romantic ruin'. Stone from the ruins found its way into the homes and public houses of Titchfield. However, the roofless outer structure and foundations of the out-buildings remained and can be visited to this day. Sections of late medieval tile floor work are amongst the more rare architectural features on this site. Each room and part of the structure has an information board explaining its purpose and function. In recent years the abbey has been used for concerts, *son et lumiere* presentations and Shakespearean re-enactments.
www.astoft.co.uk/titchfieldabbey.htm

20: Solent Shores: along the coastal path from Hillhead to Thatchers Coppice

Sea breezes – Southampton Water shipping – International bird sanctuary

Distance	5.6 miles
Approximate time	Three hours
Start and finish	Titchfield Haven foreshore car park (western end) by Meon Road at Hillhead. 4 miles south of Titchfield via the A27. Grid reference 531023
Refreshments	See Walk 19
Map	OS 1:25,000 Explorer Sheet 119 Meon Valley

This route involves easy walking on level and broad permissive and public paths that often follow the line of farm access tracks. Much of the walk is through and around the protected Chilling Coastal Area and Brownwich Farms Estate. In the 1960s the Hampshire County Council deliberately purchased some 1200 acres of land in this area to protect the coast from urban development and to preserve wildlife habitats. Much of the land is actively farmed by tenant farmers growing wheat, barley, sweetcorn and leaf vegetables such as cabbages. At an earlier time, strawberry growing was on a big scale. The coastal part of the walk enjoys superb views of the central Solent across to Cowes on the Isle of Wight and the lower part of Southampton Water. There is a need to exercise care on the coastal path. The cliffs vary in height from 15-40 feet and the edge is unfenced and liable to crumble as the underlying clays are very soft.

Note that some of the permissive paths are not marked on the OS Sheet 119 Meon Valley. These paths are clearly signed in the field with waymarks and signposts.

1. **From the road sign 'Meon Shore' follow the path signed 'Footpath Only. No horses' as it passes behind the rather curious group of beach-front chalets.**

   At the end of these chalets take the path up the low cliff and walk ahead with bushes on the left and property fences on the right. Very soon, at the end of the property fence, stop at the break in the bushes to take in the first full view of the seascape.

   There are usually oil tankers moored at the jetties at Fawley Refinery. Southampton Water is alive with ferries, container ships, small craft and more often than not, the world's most famous cruise liners. Directly opposite is Calshot Spit, the base for the historic Schneider Air Races that were part of the international sporting calender prior to World War II and which contributed to the development of the Spitfire.

2. **Continue along the cliff path.**

Solent Shores: the route passes along the top of the cliffs beyond Hillhead

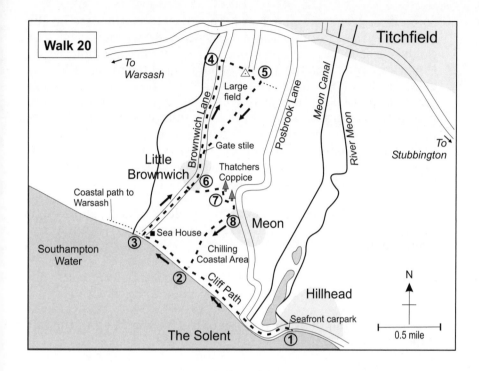

From time to time breaks in the bushes on the left provide great viewing points. To the right are the farmlands of the Chilling Coastal Area.

Just before Sea House, take the left fork in the path to descend to the foreshore.

This is a good spot for a bit of beachcombing and pond exploration. The overflow from Brownwich Pond, a little way inland, flows into the sea here through some intriguing little lagoons and marshland.

3. **Just past Sea House, leave the shore to turn right (inland) at the gate. This quickly becomes a broad vehicle access track. Go through the gate at Lower Brownwich Farm and walk ahead in a northerly direction on the concreted farm track. Continue past Little Brownwich Farm.**

Soon, pass properties and Thornton Nursery glass houses on the left as the track becomes more obviously Brownwich Lane. The fields hereabouts and the woods around the watercourses in Hookgate Coppice to the left are much frequented by birds. This is great for the walker and the birdwatcher. It is probably not so great for hard-pressed farmers as the birds set about the seedlings and plants in these arable fields. If you have children with you get them to try and spot at least ten species in this vicinity. This is a haunt of skylarks, seagulls, robins, blue tits, crows, collared doves, wood pigeons, mallard ducks, pheasants, starlings, blackbirds and Canada geese amongst other species.

4. **At the end of the open farmland, by modern houses, go through the gate. In 200 yards turn right at the yellow waymarked fingerpost.**

This path quickly takes on the character of a 'canopied grotto' with over-arching bushes, creepers and ivy and evergreen shrubs.

Cross a stile and another one beyond it as you keep to the left hand edge of two fields.

These are sheep paddocks and, depending on the time of year, you may be surrounded by fat lambs! Look to your right for long views down to The Solent which often shimmers in the sunshine when viewed on a fine day from this place.

At the incongruously and inexplicably located concrete trig column in the corner of the field turn right.

5. **Cross the stile at the next fingerpost on the left to exit the field. Turn right and almost immediately left on a broad track. In 100 yards, at the 'three-way' fingerpost, turn right. In a further 100 yards enter an enormous field which stretches away to the south.**
   On the OS map (Sheet 119 Meon Valley) the path veers to the right to cross this field at an angle. However, you will see by the fence on the right a 'Permissive Footpath' sign. Follow this as it directs you firstly across the top of the field and then left to parallel Brownwich Lane on your right. In the bottom right-hand

corner rejoin Brownwich Lane through the gated stile.You are now back on the line of your outward route.

6. Just after re-passing Little Brownwich farm, leave the outward route by turning left at the powerline pole. This pole has a blue off-road cycle route indicator on it. Walk ahead on this concrete track to Thatchers Coppice.

7. Leave the concrete and take the signed footpath through the coppice to the public car park.

There is a signboard here which explains the work of Hampshire County Council and Brownwich Farms Estate in managing the Chilling Coastal Area. The names of butterflies and birds that frequent the coppice are listed on the board also.

   Thatchers Coppice is a fragment of old forest in which the traditional form of tree farming known as coppicing was and is still practised. A further feature to look out for here are the aerial 'runways' – cross branches of hazel trees encouraged to grow transversely about 15 feet above ground level to help rare dormice to skip from habitat to habitat. No doubt the numerous squirrels in this wood use them also.

8. With your back to the signboard, walk across the car park to join the footpath on the other side and continue through the coppice.
   Leave Thatchers Coppice over a small wooden footbridge. Go left and immediately right and walk straight ahead on the fenced footpath between large fields to the cliff-top path. Cross the stile and turn left onto your original route back to Hillhead.

By the Way

Titchfield Haven National Nature Reserve
This is an internationally recognised and protected nature reserve of 369 acres at the mouth of the Meon River. The river completes its 21 mile journey by reaching the sea through several square miles of watermeadows, reedbeds, marshes, wetlands, and lagoons impounded behind the shingle banks of the Solent shore. The river once flowed to the sea through an open estuary. However the river mouth was enclosed by dykes and banks in 1611 to create agricultural areas

upstream that were less susceptible to inundation. The river now flows out into the sea through a culvert and controlled sluices into the small and pretty Hillhead harbour which dries out at low tide.

Some 200 species of bird have been sighted and recorded in the reserve. The lagoons and reedbeds especially are home and feeding ground to large numbers of wading birds and migratory species from places as far afield as Siberia. There are avocets, bearded tits, oyster catchers, bitterns, reed warblers,

The Titchfield Haven National Nature Reserve

several species of duck, water rails, moorhens, and large flocks of geese. Daily sightings of birds, especially the rarer visitors, are chalked up on a notice board just inside the visitor centre. These often cause great excitement amongst the regular birdwatchers at this site. Dotted about the reserve are well-constructed hides which permit both serious birdwatchers and the casual visitor alike to observe the variety of bird life. There is a charge to access the hides and boardwalks in the waterlands.

The visitor centre contains the Haven Tea Rooms with fine views across the Solent to the Isle of Wight. Here also, in an exhibition space, are wall-charts of the reserve explaining its conservation and habitat management functions; and hands-on displays particularly suitable for young children. The Gallery shows monthly exhibitions of artwork by local and national artists on nature themes. There is a shop selling natural history books, locally crafted items such as turned wood artifacts, conservation products, and supplies of bird food. Information on wildlife sightings is provided and binoculars can be hired for those wishing to view the birds from the hides.

www.hants.gov.uk/titchfield Ph 01329 662145

Answers to Walk 15 Quiz

Q1. Grey Wagtail. Kingfisher. Great Tit. Kestrel. Great Spotted
     Woodpecker. Long Tailed Tit.
Q2. The Roebuck.
Q3. Sarum.
Q4. M.
Q5. Three.
Q6. Golf course sand bunker.
Q7. Wooden, ornamental spiked gates.
Q8. Usually two of at least four, depending on sight lines through
     the trees.
Q9. Mainly oaks.
Q10. At least eleven, depending on visibility.
Q11. Tick any one of the following: Climbing invasive ivy; Beefsteak
     fungus; Razor Strop fungus;Tinder fungus, depending on the
     time of year.
Q12. Cupola clock tower on the main hospital building; open cross
     towerette on the preserved chapel.
Q13. Wastewater treatment works.
Q14. Knowle Junction.
Q15. Pinkish or light fawn.
Q16. Sluices and overflow channels.
Q17. Wooden bench.
Q18. Three.
Q19. Mayles Close.
Q20. Twenty six or twenty seven depending on where you start the
     count.

Also from Sigma Leisure:

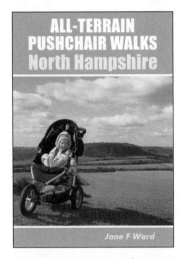
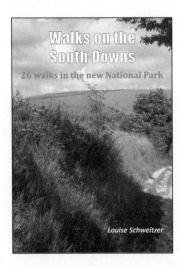